Backpackers' Ultra Food

BACKPACKERS' ULTRA FOOD

More than 50 Ultra Light, Ultra Delicious,
Ultra Nutritious One-Pot Backpacking Meals

Cinny Green

Author of the award-winning *Trail Writer's Guide*

Western Edge Press   -   Santa Fe

ISBN: 978-889921-51-8
Library of Congress Control Number: 2013934557

Sherman Asher Publishing
126 Candelario St.
Santa Fe, NM 87501
www.shermanasher.com

Design by Jim Mafchir
Drawings by Chris Riedel
Cover background photo by Ana June
Cover food photo by Carolyn Lake, prepared by Patti Lentz
Edited by Barbara Feller-Roth

Manufactured in the U.S.A.

Acknowledgments

So much assistance and affirmation went into the creation of this work. I would like to thank Jim Mafchir, publisher of Western Edge Press, for his thorough support of this project and also for the endlessly inspiring stories of his international backcountry adventures.

Many thanks to my companions on the 2012 Santa Fe/Taos Women's Backpacking Adventure who embraced the concept of ultra food and were nourished on our ten-day trek by the dishes they made from my recipes. I heard many hungry lip-smacking sounds of pleasure as they tasted their nightly meals. Thank you fellow hikers Carolyn Lake, Patti Lentz, Ana Junc, Theresa Ferraro, Kristin Barendsen, and Renee Gonyier. Grace Berge was our video instructor and she joined us for several days of the excursion along with Mercedes Marchand, our trek sponsor from Goodhew/Sockwell, crafters of superior and innovative lifestyle socks. We could not have walked all those miles without her remarkable socks as well as good food.

I am grateful to Chris Riedel for his gracious and outstanding backup support of the Santa Fe/Taos adventure and the exceptional meals he prepared at our resupply stop. He also created the illustrations that invite the reader into the pages of this book.

Many thanks to Barbara Feller-Roth for her excellent editing and shared love of the trail.

Finally, the Great Wild Mother Earth has my ever present and undying gratitude for simply being.

Contents

On the Trail   3

The Body and Backpacking   7

The Lightweight Camp Kitchen   19

Ultra Foods for Backpackers   29

Ultra Meals for the Trail   41

Backpackers' Pantry   61

Trail Snacks   65

Backcountry Breakfasts   71

Backcountry Lunches   77

Backcountry Dinners   81

Delectable Desserts   97

Packaging Food for a Hike   101

Trail's End   105

Notes   106

References   110

Index   112

Don't eat anything your great grandmother wouldn't recognize as food.

—Michael Pollan

Backpackers' Ultra Food

On the Trail

It has been eight hours since breakfast and four hours since a quick lunch of hummus and crackers. Nuts, seeds, dried fruit, jerky, and chocolate provided energy for three to four miles of switchbacks up to the ridge at 12,000 feet. The six miles along the alpine tundra, with 360-degree views, were exceptional.

Below a small cirque, there is a lake surrounded by tall pines: the day's destination. After a steep but short descent, a path leads me through a meadow to a grove near the shallow green lake. There is a ring of charred stones for a fire circle and plenty of dead branches. Soon my tent rests on a bed of soft pine needles with the door opening to the east; an inflated pad and inviting sleeping bag cover the floor. Nearby, my backpack hangs on a lower branch, and on the other side of the grove, a bear bag rope dangles between two trees waiting for the laden food sack. The fire is crackling, making a nice layer of orange coals.[1] A big log next to the hearth offers a perfect backrest. The pressing question: what is for dinner?

Hiking in backcountry is not an athletic event. It is, however, an endeavor that burns a lot of calories and demands sustained physical effort. If it is cold or rainy, the effort is even more demanding. And nothing is more alluring or more desired after a hard day on the trail than a hot, filling, flavorful meal eaten as dusk surrounds the campsite and quiet settles over the wilderness.

I am not a nutritionist. I am a hiker who loves to go into the backcountry for days—and I love to eat. In the process of experimenting with assorted trail food strategies and learning over many years what constitutes "healthy" food, I've come up with backpackers' ultra food: home-prepared meals made of the tastiest, lightest, most nourishing and restorative food. These "one-pot wonders" satisfy a hiker's need for a spectacular meal at the end of the day. Beyond being tasty, these dishes provide the exceptional nourishment that you have earned.

In formulating these At Home and In Camp cooking strategies and recipes, I have relied on six essential criteria for creating exceptional trail food for hikers:

1. Ultra foods. Certain meats, seafood, poultry, vegetables, fruits, grains, nuts, and seeds provide specific nutrients based on the task at hand. For backpackers this means replenishing those parts of the body that have worked the hardest: muscles, joints, heart, lungs, and other organs involved in directly feeding the body during sustained exercise.

2. Plenty of calories. Hiking is sustained exertion—sometimes light, sometimes heavy, but always constant. In an average day, you burn about 100 calories an hour. On an average backpacking trip when you're carrying 20 pounds or more, you burn as much as 500 calories an hour.[2]

3. Lightweight food. Without sacrificing flavor, calories, or nutrition, the backpacker should carry about two pounds of food per person per day. The basic tools for making these simple, light meals are dehydrating and forethought.

4. Lightweight cooking utensils. Any hike can become a complete slog if your pack is too heavy. Follow ultralight guidelines[3] when purchasing equipment and you'll sail along the trail, as well as know you have all the necessities for preparing fabulous food.

5. Simplicity of preparation. After eight to ten hours of sustained exertion, a tired hiker does not need the aggravation of complicated recipes, tangled bags of food, or undercooked or overcooked glop. The *Backpackers' Ultra Food* recipes are almost all one-pot meals with just a few steps in preparation.

6. Reward for a mission accomplished. Backpacking has very particular challenges that require heightened attention all day, and a great meal is a terrific celebration and the best form of relaxation. The ultra food pantry offers an array of spices that replenish your body as well as season your dinner with classic and ethnic blends. *Salud!*

Perhaps it seems like a colossal impossibility to meet all these criteria. Surely, you think, if the food is going to be textured and flavorful, it won't be lightweight or easy to prepare. A rewarding exceptional meal must need extra pots and pans and a cabinet of seasonings. Carbo-loading is the only way to get tons of calories and lots of quick energy. Out in the wilderness, you do the best you can to feed your body but worry about the perfect balance of all those vitamins and minerals back home.

Wrong!

So, what does it take to make this "ultra" food? It takes a simple knowledge of the foods and spices that are packed with the nutrients needed to revitalize the body; meals with plenty of calories for the lightest weight; delicious texture and flavors; easy one-pot menus in simple packaging; and quick preparation. This book has put all that information in one place so you can peruse these pages and adapt the recipes for your preferences and taste.

These recipes, although easy, do require prep time in the kitchen before you hit the trail. The payoff is maximum nutrition and flavor when you most need it. As you imagine where you will be when you actually savor these meals—the wild—your time in the kitchen can give you great pleasure and the confidence that your body will be revved for the next adventure.

I build up my stash of meals over months, especially the long winter months, so the prep isn't rushed and anxious as hiking season approaches. And as I'm packaging my grains, veggies, jerky, and trail mix, I image all the stunning backcountry settings where you and I will be enjoying these ultra breakfasts, snacks, lunches, dinners, and desserts.

The Body and Backpacking

Physical activity is beneficial for most people, both those suffering from illness as well as those who are healthy. It can lead to weight loss and it improves mood as well as cardiac, respiratory, and muscular functions. Whether you are walking around the block or running up a mountain, the proper diet plays a huge role in making exercise feel good. During the fifteen years I lived on an organic farm and later researched and wrote about healing foods, I learned that food grown locally, organic when possible, and humanely raised on rich soil provides maximum nutrition. The following information is my layperson's understanding of nutrition and the body. It is not heavy on numbers. The concepts are based on general nutritional studies out in the world, available to everyone.[4]

If you aren't interested in biochemistry-lite, then skip to the next chapter. Suffice it to say, I don't believe in ultra control: low-this, high-that, you'll-die-if-you-eat-x, miracle-cure diet plans. You simply need carbohydrates, protein, and fats as well as micronutrients from real food to keep you going on the trail.

What happens when you exercise?

Macronutrients for the human body are carbohydrates (CHO), fats, and protein from food. The concept is simple: to sustain activity, energy must be supplied to muscles at about the same rate it is used up. When the rate of supply exceeds the rate of use, you gain weight. When the rate of use exceeds the supply, you feel fatigue or, in the long run, lose weight. The power station is the mitochondria of your muscle cells where CHOs and fat are "burned" with the help of oxygen. Called aerobic metabolism, it is the primary energy source for any exercise lasting more than a minute or two.

Carbohydrates

CHOs are stored in muscles and the liver as glycogen, which becomes glucose, or blood sugar. The liver supplies a steady stream of glucose to keep all systems fed, especially the brain. Muscles have about three times as much glycogen as the liver to support activity, but it becomes depleted during exercise lasting longer than sixty to ninety minutes. That is not enough time for a marathon or a soccer match or a daylong hike in the wilderness. When the CHOs are used up, the body will begin burning fats, but it is a much slower process and will literally slow you down, an obvious limitation for athletic effort. It can also make your muscles ache and subdue your mood. Low blood sugar becomes a serious problem in the backcountry when a hiker's brain runs out of glycogen (hypoglycemia) and can't problem-solve clearly. That can become a life-threatening situation.

There are two ways to increase your ability to maintain energy while exercising. One is improving the way oxygen burns your fuel—making a more efficient power plant. Aerobic training (exercising to improve your system's ability to get oxygen from your lungs and blood to your muscles) helps fat metabolize faster so the limited glycogen in muscles and the liver is spared until absolutely needed. Aerobic training also helps metabolize the stored glycogen. Every hiker, especially a distance hiker, benefits from regular aerobic exercise, whether it is fast walking, cycling, running, regular incline hiking, or versions of those at the gym on the treadmill, elliptical machine, or stationary bike, or in an aerobics class. All of these improve the volume of oxygen that runs through your system to ignite energy. You breathe deeper and faster, expanding your lungs to get oxygen into the system. Your blood vessels increase in diameter so oxygen and nutrients can be delivered swiftly to the muscles. You strengthen the muscles of your heart so it can pump faster.

Some long-distance hikers wait to get "fit" over the first days on the trail itself, but it makes more sense to maintain steady fitness so you are trail-ready on the day you leave. You'll still have plenty of challenges because there is no training that can exactly prepare you for the demands on muscles that change with footing, distance, incline, decline, altitude, temperature, and speed on a backcountry trail.

The other way to improve your energy metabolism is diet—selecting the best fuel for your power plant. First, eating well prior to exercise is as important as aerobic training. Researchers in sports nutrition have learned that the first goal for endurance is to make sure the competitor consumes plenty of CHOs in advance to fill the storage units in the muscles and liver to the max. In one study, endurance runners improved their pace by 25 percent after consuming a high-CHO diet for three days before the race. Another study showed that runners ran faster after eating a high-CHO diet for seven days.[5]

A normal ratio for consumption of macronutrient calories is 40 percent CHOs, 30 percent protein, and 30 percent fat each day. A simple guideline before hitting the trail for a long, hard hike would be to add another 10 percent of CHOs daily a week beforehand to maximize energy. So your ratio would be more like 50:25:25. It is not rocket science, and, like most folks, I do not normally count or measure my macros. I shoot for a classic daily balance of meat or fish, veggies and grains, and fats and oils. Individual bodies vary in metabolism, so experiment to find your best ratio.

Replacing depleted glycogen in the muscles and liver is also important, especially right after exercise. Eat within one and a half to two hours after exercise when your system is still humming from exertion, and your recovery rate will be swift and sure. Eat a highly nutritious meal full of CHOs, protein, and good fats as well as plenty of other nutrients such as vitamins, minerals, and all those mystery micronutrients in fresh foods. Scientists know a little about what each nutrient does by itself, but they are just beginning to understand how they operate in tandem. We intuitively know that the more nutrient rich our food, the better we feel and the better we are able to take on the physical challenges that matter to us.

Protein

Proteins are the building blocks of the human body. Made up of amino acids, they help build muscles, blood, skin, hair, nails, and internal organs. Next to water, protein is the most plentiful substance in the body, and about 60 to 70 percent of it is located in the skeletal muscles. Because endurance athletes tend to focus on CHO intake to improve endurance, they sometimes neglect the need for protein, thinking that protein is for the weight lifters buffing up their muscle mass. Yet the maintenance, repair, and growth of lean muscle depend on protein, which is the primary substance of muscle and promotes a healthy immune system. Without protein, you become vulnerable to fatigue, lethargy, anemia, and even more severe disorders. You don't want insufficient protein to get in the way of your joy of being in the wilderness.

If you feel very sore after a long day on the trail, you might lack enough protein in your diet. After about ninety minutes of exercise, muscle glycogen stores become nearly depleted. The body begins to synthesize glucose from the fatty acids and amino acids of lean muscle tissue. It is a kind of cannibalizing to find more fuel. The remedy is to make sure you eat protein—along with your CHOs—all day and especially at the end of the day so you can undo the damage and stress and refill your cellular storage facility.

Whey and soy supplements are the endurance athlete's choice of protein, but as a hiker I believe in focusing on real foods because they contain all the companion nutrients that have been processed out of supplements—or perhaps put back piecemeal. Grass-fed lean meats such as poultry, beef, buffalo, and lamb provide excellent protein. Marinated jerky tastes great and is light in weight. But variety as well as caloric value are important, so I always have high-quality nuts such as almonds, walnuts, and cashews in my trail mix, and I eat some nut butter, hard cheese, or foil-packed or dehydrated tuna for lunch.

In the evening, it is extremely important to eat a meal with a good source of protein as well as those highly praised carbs—especially within two hours of ceasing high activity. No white-flour spaghetti and tomato sauce for me! Pack meals with various combos of protein: meat, poultry, salmon, or tuna; quinoa, beans, soy, or other whole grains; and/or a little dairy. Applying forethought to the recipe makes it easy to provide near-perfect recovery nutrition in homemade trail food.

Fats

Much attention is paid to the role of CHOs and protein in muscle performance and fatigue, but fats shouldn't be neglected. Fat has a bad reputation as the culprit of weight gain and disease because it contains more calories per gram. But we need those extra calories on the trail. What is important is to distinguish between good fats versus bad fats, and they may not be what you think.

Whether your preferred fat—or any food—is vegetable or animal based, the least processed from the healthiest source is always the healthiest nutrient. As nutrition writer Michael Pollan says, "You are what you grow."[6] So start with the freshest, least processed version of your fat of choice.

After years of going round and round about what is bad or good about fats, here is what scientists have come to understand: reducing fat in our diets is not necessarily a good thing, and it won't necessarily prevent disease or promote sustainable weight loss. In fact, the more the food industry has tried to formulate processed fat alternatives, rates of heart disease—and most other degenerative diseases such as cancer, diabetes, and arthritis—have soared. In 1920, heart disease was rare; now it causes 40 percent of all deaths. Fat is blamed, but it isn't the culprit.[7] It is all about the kind of fat in addition to, of course, too much refined sugar and huge portions.

How can you distinguish one fat from another and know how much to eat? Fats from animal and vegetable sources provide an important natural source of energy as well as build cell membranes and stimulate a variety of hormones. Fats in a meal slow down absorption so that we can go longer without feeling hungry. In addition, they carry essential fat-soluble vitamins A, D, E, and K to tissue and are needed for a bundle of other processes. Mother's milk contains over 50 percent of its calories as fat. Both cholesterol and saturated fat are essential for growth in babies, especially in the developing brain.

But as you get older, saturated fats such as butter, eggs, milk, and cheese are bad for you, right? In the 1950s, a researcher named Ancel Keys proposed a link between saturated fat in the diet, high cholesterol, and heart disease. The media promoted this theory, doctors jumped on board, the food industry formulated whole new lines of low-fat products and substitutes, and cholesterol drugs became a billion-dollar cash cow for pharmaceutical companies. (It has been suggested that they formulated the cholesterol-lowering medication first and had to invent a reason to sell it.) Saturated Fat Is Bad became a dietary religion, perpetuated in spite of the fact that the most famous forty-year longitudinal study on diet, the Framingham study, concluded the following: "The people in the study who ate the most cholesterol, ate the most saturated fat, ate the most calories weighed the least and were the most physically active."[8] That just blows my mind after fifty-plus years of propaganda to the contrary.

Here is mind-blower number two: Studies could sometimes make a connection between so-called good dietary habits—reduced saturated fat and cholesterol, reduced smoking, weight loss, and so on—and a slight decrease in coronary heart disease, but the overall mortality of the participants in the studies from all causes—such as cancer, stroke, even suicide and violent death—went up. What? Stop eating saturated fat and your likelihood of dying from other causes actually increases. Why? The answer is that the rates of all those diseases have risen as fast as heart disease in the last century. If one doesn't get you, another one will. And the rise in all chronic diseases indisputably parallels the amount of over-processed food made with toxic trans fats (formulated to save us from saturated fats) as well as excessive calories, minimal nutrients, inflammatory sugars, and additives. On the other hand, studies of Mediterranean, Eskimo, Soviet Georgian, Swiss, Austrian, Yemenite Jewish, South Asian, Chinese, and Japanese cultures demonstrate that diets based on moderate consumption of animal fats correlate with reduced rates of degenerative diseases and greater longevity.[9]

There is a connection between fats and heart disease, though. Fatty-acid chains in the blood, called triglycerides, are positively linked to a tendency toward heart disease. Triglycerides are a form of fat, but those associated with heart disease apparently do not come directly from dietary fats. They are made in the liver from consumed sugars that have not been used to produce energy.[10] The source of these sugars is any food containing carbohydrates, including refined sugar and white flour. This suggests that chronic disease may be primarily a sugar problem, not a saturated fat problem.

All fats and oils, whether of vegetable or animal origin, are some combination of saturated fatty acids, monounsaturated fatty acids, and polyunsaturated fatty acids. It is not easy to juggle all this contradictory info about which fats are best. However, I have learned that it is really important to eat good fats to stay nourished and healthy on the trail. So here is a short course in these three forms of fatty acids.

Saturated: A fatty acid is saturated when all the carbon-atom linkages are filled—or saturated—with hydrogen. They are highly stable, even when heated for cooking, and they rarely go rancid. They form a solid or semisolid fat at room temperature. Your body makes saturated fatty acids from carbohydrates, and they are also found in animal fats and tropical oils. In general, animal fats such as butter contain about 40 to 60 percent saturated fat. Coconut oil is 92 percent saturated. Ghee (see page 63) and Parmesan cheese are ideal choices of saturated fat in trail meals. One ounce of Parmesan has

12 percent of the recommended daily value for fat and 21 percent for protein.[11] Now that is a backpacker's ultra food.

Monounsaturated: Monounsaturated fatty acids have one double carbon bond lacking two hydrogen atoms. They tend to be liquid at room temperature. They don't go rancid easily and can be used in cooking. The monounsaturated fatty acid most commonly found in our food is oleic acid, the main component of olive oil as well as the oils from almonds, pecans, cashews, peanuts, and avocados. Take a small quantity of olive oil in your trail pantry for delicious pesto, tabouli, and hummus. Eat nuts and nut butter, too.

Polyunsaturated: Polyunsaturated fatty acids have two or more pairs of double carbon bonds and lack four or more hydrogen atoms. The two polyunsaturated fatty acids found most frequently in our foods are double unsaturated linoleic acid—also called omega-6— and triple unsaturated linolenic acid—also called omega-3. A 2:1 ratio between them is the most nutritious. These fatty acids are called "essential" because your body cannot make them; you have to get them from food. They go rancid easily, particularly omega-3s, and should never be heated or used in cooking. They are liquid even when refrigerated. Common polyunsaturated fats are corn, soy, canola, and cottonseed oils. The ways these are typically processed destroys omega-3s, so be sure to get "expeller pressed" or "cold pressed" versions. Products with the best ratios of omega-6 to omega-3 are flaxseed oil, fish oil (especially krill), nuts, and seeds. Nuts are an ideal backpackers' source of these oils, as are foil-packed or dehydrated tuna and salmon.

Trans fats: Polyunstaturated fats such as corn, soy, canola, and cottonseed oil are the most unstable fatty acids. Because they go rancid quickly, food producers discovered a way—hydrogenation—to turn them into solid margarine and shortening. The process of "transforming" these fats is full of heavy metals, dyes, and additives, which turn them into toxic sludge, not food. In spite of that danger, they continue to be sold as a "healthy" alternative to saturated fats and are commonly used in fast food fryers because they can be used over and over. The fats from these products lodge in your cells and are associated with a host of diseases such as cancer, low-birth-weight babies, autoimmune diseases, and heart disease. Quite simply, eating dirt is probably safer than ingesting hydrogenated vegetable oils. (Don't do either, of course.)

General guidelines for fats

What does all this mean for the humble, hungry backpacker? You need fat for steady energy. You need good fat that travels through the bloodstream with other nutrients to rebuild your tired muscles. You need fats that won't go rancid. Based on the short course in fatty acids, you need saturated fats, such as cheese, coconut oil, ghee (clarified butter, which does not need to be refrigerated); meat; monounsaturated fats, such as olive oil; and minimally processed polyunsaturated fats, such as raw nuts, nut butters, and fish. Let processed polyunsaturated fats and trans fats fester on grocery store shelves until the producers realize we know better than to eat such rancid toxic products.

An active ingredient in olive oil—oleic acid—is also a known anti-inflammatory as well as one of the healthiest fats on the planet. One tablespoon a day is enough to meet your basic need for this cartilage builder. Olive oil can really help your sustained energy and your recovery from a hard day on the trail. Use extra-virgin, cold-pressed varieties because heat isn't used in the extraction process so the oil retains its beneficial nutrients. Keep it cool next to the water bladder in your backpack.

Nuts are a staple of backpackers' trail mix because of protein; the essential fatty acids, vitamins, and minerals are an extra bonus. Every hour or two when I eat dried fruit for quick sugar energy, I drop a nut or two in my mouth to keep a nice balance of the three fundamental foods: CHOs, protein, and fat. A dark chocolate chip helps a lot, too!

Cheese is full of vitamins as well as saturated fat and protein. Softer cheeses tend to mold without refrigeration, so I take 4 to 8 ounces of hard cheese such as Parmesan or Asiago. They last an extra day or so. I also experiment with dehydrated shredded hard cheese, which makes a tasty crispy topping or cheesy sauce when rehydrated with whole milk powder and ghee.

Eggs are another natural source of fat. They were also vilified by the Saturated Fat Is Bad dietary religion. Yet eggs provide protein, iron, calcium, and vitamin A, making them a top-notch balanced fuel for endurance activity and recovery. Hard-boiled eggs can last a day or two without refrigeration.

Fluids

The next component for healthy endurance is water, which comprises about 60 percent of your body weight. As you exercise, you sweat and lose fluids through your skin, and you need to replace them so your blood is fluid enough to carry oxygen and nutrients around your body. Depending on the ambient temperature and the intensity of exercise, you may need between a cup and a quart of water per hour. Drinking small amounts steadily throughout exertion keeps you hydrated so nutrients can flow to their intended destinations. (That is why I love water bladders with tubing. I sip every ten to fifteen minutes on the trail, especially before an incline.)

Dehydration contributes to cramps and injuries on many levels. Inattention about intake of fluids can cause you to make painful mistakes. If your body fluids are down by just a half liter, your endurance may be reduced by about 20 percent, and oxygen uptake through your heart and lungs drops about 20 percent. Water also helps to lubricate your joints so you move with greater ease.

If you are feeling thirsty, you are already somewhat dehydrated. Because the body often doesn't register thirst until you are already dehydrated, do not rely on this as the sole indicator of dehydration. The other warning signs of dehydration include:

Muscle cramping
Headaches
Dry mouth
Unclear thinking

Hydration is especially critical in the backcountry because your survival depends not just on fitness but on good judgment. Whenever you find yourself lapsing in clarity, STOP! EAT! DRINK! REST! Don't move on until you feel strong and clear.

Recently I led a group on a multi-day trip through the Rockies. Two women suffered dehydration because they didn't want to drink all their water before they got to the next source, even though they had full containers. This lapse in judgment, exacerbated by the lack of water, resulted in one getting sick to her stomach and the other getting wobbly legs on a decline. Ingesting a quick two cups of water with some nourishing snacks remedied both. And the experiences were enough to make them rehydrate continually for the rest of the trip.

Electrolytes are critical, too. They help maintain the fluid/mineral balance in your cells and prevent symptoms of dehydration. Electrolytes are micronutrients, including sodium, potassium, magnesium, and calcium, that form and carry the electrical energy necessary for muscle contractions and transmission of nerve impulses, as well as other functions. Our miraculous body requires a regular supply of these important nutrients. Our bodies are also wired to maintain just the right balance of electrolytes, so unless you are cycling the Tour de France or running the New York City Marathon (feats that defy the body's natural exert/rest/nourish cycles), good food and plenty of water will do the job.

The extreme sports industry offers a host of products marketed to those of us who participate in more basic physical challenges. The simplest, wisest way to sustain the body on the trail is to STOP! EAT! DRINK! REST! regularly, not just in crisis. Do not wait until you hurt or feel sick before you refuel with food and replenish fluids, including electrolyte-rich ingredients. To avoid the unnecessary additives of packaged sports drinks, eat foods high in natural, essential electrolytes. Are they hard to find? Absolutely not! They include such staples as salt, citrus, nuts, and leafy vegetables. See the Trail Snacks section for more choices and details.

In summary, you can sustain your energy level on a long hike by ingesting regular amounts of CHOs, protein, fat, micronutrients, and water as you go along. Keep a balanced trail mix within easy reach, and be sure to stop for a nourishing lunch. In anticipation of higher demands such as a steep incline or skipping down a path to get off a ridge in a lightning storm, eat some quickly absorbed sugar, such as dried fruit, with a gulp of water. These strategies will maintain glucose levels, burn fat, slow the depletion of glycogen in your liver, postpone the cannibalizing of muscles, and keep all nutrients flowing smoothly throughout your body.

Every system—digestive, respiratory, circulatory, muscular-skeletal—is involved in exercise. Their collective response is a chorus of heart, blood vessels, nerves, lungs, digestive organs, and skin. Sometimes it sounds like a low hum; sometimes it is a crescendo, especially when you just made it up to a ridge or a summit and the wind hits your face. It feels so good.

The Lightweight Camp Kitchen

M ost of the gear I originally purchased for hiking sits in the back of my closet, and I pull it out only when visitors come to hike and don't have any equipment. It is good stuff but not quite the most efficient for my purposes.

Over the last several years, I've tried lots of ultralight gizmos, from backpacks to clothing to knives. My primary caveats for all purchases were and are that—in order of importance—the items make me safe, prepared for emergencies, and comfortable. Most of the products have certainly kept me safe and prepared for emergencies. Not all were as comfortably lightweight as I needed. Products are as varied as the personalities of people who use them, and the backpacking industry updates them from season to season.

This list is primarily intended to let you know what criteria I use to select items for my personal camp kitchen. There will soon be lighter and better ones, devices that are made of recycled and sustainable materials, but these are my necessities of choice for food preparation in the backcountry.

Water purification

Paying attention to your water consumption is essential for hydration. Because many trailside water sources are contaminated, it is best to carry a water-purification device or be prepared to boil water.

There are several reasons why it is not safe to drink straight out of many streams, lakes, springs, and other trailside water sources. Many are contaminated by pesticides, herbicides, and fertilizers as well as viruses, bacteria, and other organic parasites. Many water sources contain chemical contamination from pesticide runoff, mine tailings, industrial effluence, and fertilizers. Boiling, filtering, and chemically treating water can remove or kill microorganisms, but they cannot remove chemical toxins. So I try not to hike downstream from a plastics factory, paper mill, or nuclear power plant.

Biologically contaminated water contains pathogens such as *Giardia lamblia* and *Cryptosporidium*, which lead to intestinal disorders, as well as bacteria or viruses that can lead to infections. There are four common ways to purify biologically contaminated water in the backcountry: boiling, chemical purification, filters, and ultraviolet (UV) light.[12] A water filter can remove biological contaminants, protozoa, parasites, and bacteria, but most do not remove viruses. A water purifier eliminates those contaminants as well as viruses. Check the labels, though, because these products are improved every year.

Boiling: This is the traditional means of removing microorganisms from water, but for the long-distance hiker, it can be impractical because it uses extra fuel. Nonetheless, it is easy, and it will get rid of all the nasty bugs that can make you sick. Simply bring the water to a rapid boil. Most organisms perish at that temperature, but for added safety continue to boil the water for one to five minutes. Add one minute to the boiling time for each thousand feet above 10,000 feet. If you have plenty of fuel, or a campfire, boil the water after dinner and let it cool overnight.

Chemical purification: Chemical treatment has improved by leaps and bounds, which is great news for the lightweight backpacker. Usually, you can add the purifier and wait thirty minutes to be protected from most pathogens. Here are some general guidelines:

1. If the water is murky, strain it through a thin cloth before treatment. A bandana works well.
2. Add the chemical to the water and swish it around to aid in dissolving.
3. Treat all parts of the container that will hold the water. Splash some of the treated water onto the lid and the threads and/or squeeze some through the hose and nozzle of your water bladder.
4. The chemicals are less effective in colder water. Double the treatment time before drinking if the water temperature is below 40°F (4°C). If needed, place the water in the sun to warm it to 60°F before treating.
5. Improve the taste of chemically treated water by pouring it back and forth between containers. Other methods include adding the following to each quart of water after it has been chemically treated: a pinch of salt, powdered vitamin C, or flavorings such as powdered lemonade mix.

Note: Read manufacturer's directions on all the following purification systems so you know what they kill and how long it takes.

Iodine—drops, tablets, or crystals—can kill most pathogens but not all, and it tastes peculiar (unless you add flavoring of choice). Iodine comes as a liquid 2 percent tincture of iodine, pure iodine crystals, or tablets such as Potable Aqua. Always store iodine in a dark container so that UV light does not reduce its effectiveness. Warning: Some people are allergic to iodine, so consult your doctor before using this purification system. (One benefit of iodine is that apparently it reduces the uptake of radioactive iodine, which is released in nuclear disasters.[13])

Chlorine kills microorganisms, but it tastes bad and has a short shelf life. Add two drops of household chlorine bleach per quart of water and let it sit for at least thirty minutes. Halazone is chlorine in tablet form. Neither chlorine nor iodine alone is completely effective against *Cryptosporidium*, although both are partially effective against *Giardia*.

Chlorine dioxide—drops or tablets—is very effective against bacteria, *Giardia*, and viruses. It tastes okay, but it takes four hours to kill the *Cryptosporidium* parasite. It is more expensive than iodine for treating large quantities of water, but for the backpacker the cost difference is negligible. Katadyn Micropur purification tablets and Aqua Mira drops and tablets are chlorine dioxide based. The Aqua Mira drop system requires mixing two components. The purification times are often shorter in newer versions of this product.

Choosing a hydration system has a lot to do with your personal drinking/hiking style. Bladders are good for quick sips on the go and constant rehydration. Although bottles can be placed in the outside pockets of your pack, they usually require you to stop to open them and drink. Whatever your preference, be sure to get high-quality plastic that is free of leaching toxins such as BPA. I find that metal bottles are too heavy for lightweight backpacking.

The bladder system for liquids is incredibly efficient. Most backpacks have interior pockets that hold one-, two-, or three-liter water bladders near your back. I have found this location keeps the water cooler than a bottle in an outside pocket and becomes a good place to keep some perishables, such as hard cheeses, relatively cool. Inside your pack, the bag hangs with the hose at the bottom for gravity feed. The tube stretches up from the bottom of the bladder through designated slits in the pack and can be slung over your shoulder and attached to your straps for easy sipping.

The flexible bladders are made of very lightweight material. There are many different sizes, and smaller ones can be used without tubes for other backpacking liquids like olive oil. When the container is empty, it lies flat and doesn't take up any dead space, as would a solid container. I prefer the wide mouth variety for ease of filling as well as inserting a UV pen to sterilize water. Brands include CamelBak and Platypus. The MSR Dromedary bags can carry up to ten liters for expeditions or long-distance dry hikes (such as in the Grand Canyon). These bags have straps that can attach to your pack, and accessories for filtration, hands-off hydration, and more.

Tip: Another good reason to use the bladder system is that water is heavy, and the best place to carry it is next to your back.

Tip: While in camp, I attach my bladder to a tree with a Velcro strap or rope so I can easily get water gravity-fed for drinking, cooking, and cleaning. The hose hangs from the bottom of the bladder just as it does in the pack.

It is wise to have at least one water bottle for a backup in case the bladder becomes punctured. Some water bottles, such as the Katadyn MyBottle water filter, are set up with cyst and carbon filters. The bottle can be filled many times. The SteriPen UV water bottle system is effective and comes with a prefilter for sediments. If you don't mind the bulk of a plastic bottle, these can be good combo systems for purification as well as drinking. Also, make sure they are made of BPA-free plastic.

When calculating your overall pack weight, remember that water weighs one pound per pint. So a full three-liter bladder weighs about six pounds, and you should drink at least that much in a day of hiking. Water is one of the heaviest items you will carry. But do not skimp! Leave behind the paperback book, cosmetics, or extra clothes so you can take as much water as needed.

Water filtration: Filters are safe, but they are heavier than chemical tablets or drops. They also can become clogged, and they can crack if dropped, so a backup chemical purifier is recommended.

Check manufacturer guidelines, but most depth filters (ceramic and charcoal) remove *Giardia, Cryptosporidium*, cholera, typhoid, amebiasis salmonella, and other pathogens. Most are not effective against viruses such as hepatitis.

Filters come in several styles: gravity filters, hand pump filters, sippy filters, and bottle filters. There are several brands of each, including Pur, MSR, Katadyn, Aqua Mira, and Timberline, and the filters come in several sizes. Filters are an evolving technology, so new products will likely be lighter and more effective.

UV purification: This lightweight germicidal ultraviolet radiation system is a handheld "pen light." When inserted into the water, it prevents microbes from reproducing unless the water is reexposed to sunlight, in which case the pathogens can reactivate. The pen light kills *Giardia* and *Cryptospridium* in a minute or two, although it takes thirty times longer to deactivate the DNA of viruses. The pen light requires batteries, so it is a good idea to carry extra, and to carry backup purification tablets in case of malfunction. Strain cloudy water to improve UV exposure. Brand names include SteriPen, Müv, Aquastar, and CamelBak.

In a perfectly equipped backpack, you'd carry a primary water purification system, such as a purification filter or a UV system, along with some chemical purifier. I used to carry a pump filter, but to reduce weight, I carried only chlorine dioxide (Aqua Mira) drops. Unfortunately when I was on a Colorado Trail seven-day hike, one of the Aqua Mira bottles cracked and spilled into the baggie, leaving me no purification system other than boiling. Fortunately I had plenty of fuel. On my next backcountry trip, I added a UV pen for filling a small drinking bottle at short stops without dealing with drops, and I carried Aqua Mira drops for my three-liter bladder when I was at longer stops.

Tip: It is a good idea to use hand sanitizer or sanitizing wipes before preparing food and eating in the wilderness. Many kill 99.9 percent of viruses and bacteria that get on your hands from various sources.

Tip: One-pot dehydrated meals for one person require one to three cups of water. It is helpful to begin rehydrating jerky and grains (and softening tougher veggies such as winter squash or sweet potatoes) at least an hour before getting to camp. I stop at the most convenient water source, purify some water, add it to the grains or jerky in a zip baggie, and then tuck the baggie back in my pack. It is a good time for a cup of tea and a cookie, too. Later, in camp, when I get my pot of water boiling, I add the softened grains and meat, which take only ten to fifteen minutes to cook.

Cooking

Camping stoves come in many shapes and styles and with various types of fuel systems. My suggestions in this book are based on preparing meals for one or two people. Be sure to check manufacturers' guidelines for use and optimum temperature ranges. Here are some of the lightest and most efficient camping stoves for lightweight backpacking: the Esbit pocket stove, canister stoves, and stoves that use liquid fuel (the most expensive of these three types).

The Esbit pocket stove burns fuel pellets in a small, fold-open metal case. This pellet stove fits easily into a daypack and weighs less than four ounces. The fuel tablet burns for about fifteen minutes and is very economical at around fifty cents each. Drawbacks are that the stove is not very windproof, so you may need to add a windscreen (aluminum foil works well), and boiling time is slow, so you may need to burn a few pellets to get your meal cooked. However, for the weight, size, and price, this is a good stove for weekend trips, ultralight fast packing,[14] or as a backup stove on the trail.

Canister stoves are my preferred system in spite of the weight of the canister and the need to pack it out. These stoves are fuel efficient, and you can get the canister size you need for the length of your hike. The separate burner simply screws on and off the canister—no spillage—and the flame is adjustable. The lightest weight burners are the Brunton Crux, Coleman Ultralight, and MSR Pocket Rocket. The burners are small, and some care needs to be taken so that the pot balances correctly, but that small drawback is well worth the weight savings.

There are versions of canister stoves called "integrated systems" in which the stove burner and pot are sold together. They pack neatly into themselves and have excellent boil times and fuel efficiency, but they can be heavier than self-chosen components. Brands include Jetboil and MRS Reactor.

Tip: There are several brands of canisters, so make sure that yours has the same threads as your burner. It is sometimes hard to find replacement canisters on long treks or in other countries. I put a fresh canister in my long-distance resupply[15] boxes so I won't get caught without a source of fuel. Make sure you have lighters, matches, or other dry, dependable fire starters. The Esbit is a good backup for the canister stove.

Tip: Now canisters can be recycled by using the Jetboil Crunchit fuel canister recycling tool.

Liquid-fuel stoves are ideal for cold weather, expeditions, and adventuring in developing countries. Unlike canister stoves, which have reduced efficiency in cold temperatures, liquid-fuel stoves perform in virtually any weather or at any elevation because a liquid-fuel stove lets you pump up the bottle to compensate, whereas a sealed fuel canister cannot be adjusted. Priming is required for liquid-fuel stoves to preheat (and vaporize) a small quantity of fuel to ensure proper ignition. The fuel is stored in metal screw-top bottles, so you can pack the precise amount of fuel you need (approximately three ounces per person per day) without having to carry extra canisters. There are several different types of liquid-fuel stoves.

White-gas stoves run on the purest, most refined fuel and burn cleaner and hotter than stoves using other liquid fuels. White gas is widely available in the United States. In a pinch, these stoves will also burn kerosene, diesel, automotive gas, aviation gas, and Stoddard solvent as well as naphtha (although manufacturers don't recommend it, and frequent cleaning is required).

Denatured alcohol stoves have few or no moving parts to worry about, weigh very little, and burn silently. I have friends who have used this heating system for years. The flame does not burn as hot as that of white gas, so it takes longer to boil water and requires more fuel. The stove has many eco-friendly advantages, though, such as being quiet and odorless, not explosive, and easily extinguished, and a recyclable plastic water bottle is adequate for transporting the fuel. Brand names include Brasslite Turbo, Caldera Cone stove system, and Trangia. You can also use a homemade soda pop can.[16] Warning: Never add alcohol to a stove that is already burning!

Tip: Bring along some aluminum foil to shape a windscreen.

Utensils

Although aluminum and plastic are very light and cheap, I prefer titanium. It costs more but it is worth it to me because it is ultralight, durable, and "biocompatible." This means it is non-toxic and not rejected by the body. Aluminum and plastic utensils have an assortment of health and sustainability issues unless you buy high end products, which are also more expensive.[17]

I have a one-liter pot and a mug made of titanium. I use the pot with its lid for two-servings meals (some might want this size for one serving). I also have a titanium spork (spoon and fork combo), which is good for scooping pasta or slurping soups. A sharp knife is also a necessity in the camp kitchen.

Tip: It really isn't essential to have titanium utensils. You can find very lightweight plastic picnic forks, knives, and spoons at any grocery store. But the beauty of Internet shopping is that you can find deals if you know what you're looking for. You also can get on your local mountaineering store e-mail list to be notified of sales or become a coop member of REI and spend your annual dividend on seeming luxuries such as titanium utensils.

Dishes

There are many outdoor bowl and plate sets. My eating bowl is a simple but elegantly designed Orikaso fold-flat camping bowl. Small origami-style flaps tuck in folds to make a three-dimensional bowl. It is a deep vessel when tucked together but completely flat when unfolded. I worried that the flaps would tend to fray or tear from use, but I've had it for four years and they show no signs of ripping. It is also easy to open flat and rinse off after eating. I tuck it into the outer pocket of my pack right next to my flat map packet. Sea To Summit also makes lightweight collapsible bowls and plates.

Tip: This Orikaso dish weighs a mere 1 1/2 ounces, so I take another that is a rectangular shape to use as an extra platter while cooking.

Ultra Foods for Backpackers

Eating the same healthy food on the trail that you eat at home is the foundation of *Backpackers' Ultra Food* recipes.[18] Although fresh fruits and veggies are heavy and deteriorate quickly without refrigeration, drying them retains about the same amount of nutrients as freezing would.

More specifically, there are foods that are very high in the micronutrients that are known to soothe pain and heal inflamed tissue. These are the same foods that nourish athletes and others who engage in endurance activities such as backpacking. You'll be surprised how common and tasty these highly nourishing foods are. Think blueberries and chocolate; imagine Indian curry and Mexican burritos.

The food producers and the media have jumped on the bandwagon with these "new" healthy foods. Food packaging touts the buzzwords "antioxidant," "vitamin C," "0 trans fats," and "fights free radicals," as well as "natural," "free-range," "wild-caught," "cage-free," and "organic." Even prestigious journals such as the *New York Times* focus on healthy eating because it has become common knowledge that our ubiquitous chronic diseases are largely a result of diets overburdened with highly processed foods. It was a simple leap for me to realize that modern "health" foods would be perfectly easy and perfectly delightful to include in my backpacking menus.

I have heard of ultralight fast-packers who eat teaspoons of white sugar for instant energy. This practice has now evolved into expensive little gel caps of glucose fatigue busters. First of all, YUK! Why eat a goo pill in the wilderness when you can suck on a sweet, tasty fig or papaya? Second, although a power pill, drink, or bar will give you brief energy, it will never serve your body better than real food.

With the growth of extreme sports has come a mountain of these products and an athletic bar set too high for most of us. Basic nutrition and reasonable goals that make the body healthier are what I mean by "ultra." Indeed, research shows that extreme training and performance may actually harm the body.[19] The human body has a wonderful vocabulary if we learn to listen. Hunger, trembling, aching muscles, hot joints, burning breath, dry mouth, pounding ears, mental confusion are all voices with wisdom if you engage in a conversation with them. Set your goals, but STOP! EAT! DRINK! REST! as your body speaks without unnecessary artificial enhancements. Then you get to hear the other voices such as moist mouth with happy tastebuds, strength in your limbs, mental clarity, and smiles.

Free-range meat, cage-free poultry, and wild fish

Protein builds muscle and provides crucial enzymes and amino acids for nearly every chemical reaction in your body. Backpackers need to consume plenty of protein in order to repair muscle tissue and provide long-lasting energy for multi-day excursions in the outdoors. Protein is digested more slowly than carbohydrates, so regular small to moderate infusions nourish best. New research shows that a protein-carbohydrate (CHO) exercise recovery meal is more effective at muscle repair than CHOs alone.[20]

Ethical principles regarding food sources are important for a backpacker. After all, the reason for going into the wilderness is precisely because it hasn't been poisoned by human waste, exploitation, and error—or at least it has been restored and protected from such abuse. We can translate this ethic into the trail food we choose.

"Cage-free" humans are healthier, and so are free-range, cage-free, and wild animals. And the food that cage-free animals provide us contains a more complete and balanced bundle of nutrients. Recent studies have found that free-range meat is higher in beta-carotene, vitamin E, omega-3s, and linoleic acid, as well as the electrolytes calcium, magnesium, and potassium—and that is the short list.[21] Furthermore, unlike the fat of feedlot animals, the fat in grass-fed meat and cage-free poultry is not full of inflammatory pollutants that lodge in your flesh. Organic plant foods are also higher in nutrients and lower in toxins than commercially grown foods.

Mercury contamination of seafood is a well-known and serious problem, and farm-raised fish offer no solution because, like all confined animals, the fish is only as healthy as its human-provided food and water. Apparently, their flesh is often full of chemical pollutants such as PCBs and DDT as well as the antibiotics needed to keep them bacteria-free in densely populated pools. Feedlot cattle, pigs, and chickens have the same problem.

Even wild warm-water fish close to shore suffer contamination from everything people flush into the water, so fish that are caught in deeper, colder offshore waters are healthier. Cold-water seafood, such as salmon, halibut, and tuna, also has more omega-3 fatty acids, which are especially important for lubrication of joints.

The dishes made from these ultra food recipes use a balance of preferably local and/or organic whole grains, fruits, and vegetables with healthy meat, poultry, or fish to blend the most replenishing, nourishing, flavorful meals in the smallest package.

Tip: If you are vegetarian, you will need to replace meat, poultry, and perhaps fish and dairy with other sources of high-quality protein. You can find plenty of great recipes in *Lipsmackin' Vegetarian Backpackin'* by Christine and Tim Connors (Three Forks Press, 2004).

Whole grains

Carbohydrates become sugar in your bloodstream, which carries the sugars throughout the body and provides quick energy. White rice, as well as breads, cereals, pasta, and crackers made from white flour, are short-term energy foods that provide an immediate boost. The problem with this highly refined family of carbohydrates is that they have been stripped of everything but their ability to raise your blood sugar as high as a Chinese rocket on the Fourth of July, with about the same lasting effects. Boom and bust. This means that you have to eat them frequently to keep up your energy and feel full. The resulting calorie load contributes to serious weight gain in sedentary people. And the processing strips out micronutrients that feed other parts of your body as you burn instant energy. It is no wonder that bad knees, hips, backs, and feet are epidemic in both athletes and nonathletes who eat primarily refined carbohydrates.

The benefit of whole grains—such as brown rice, whole wheat flour, barley, oats, couscous, quinoa, and millet—over refined grains is many tiered. They are CHOs that provide the same calories and energy as refined versions. Your liver, which converts CHOs to glycogen, doesn't really make a distinction between the sources of CHOs—it could be from a lollipop or a spelt muffin. But there are good reasons to choose the unrefined grain.

Fiber has not been stripped out in processing, and fiber has been related to lower inflammation in joints, arteries, and other internal organs. Fiber fills you up and helps release blood sugar at slow, sustained rates, giving steady energy rather than fireworks. Also, whole grains are loaded with other micronutrients that control the process of oxidation, which damages cartilage and muscles worn down through exertion. Some of those nutrients can't be released in the digestive tract without the fiber of the unrefined grain. Whole grain replenishes as it energizes rather than simply kicking you up the trail.

Some people are sensitive to gluten in grains. Here are the top seven gluten-free grains[22]:

Quinoa
Buckwheat
Millet

Amaranth
Teff
Sorghum
Wild rice

Tip: Avoid genetically modified (GMO) versions of any food. Hybrid and altered foods have been part of agribusiness for decades, but the current marriage of experimental genetic isolation of food components, the addition of toxic pesticides to the genetic makeup of food seeds, and gluttonous corporate profits have had a devastating effect on plant and animal diversity as well as the livelihood of small farmers. The impact on human health has been minimized and under-researched by business interests. More than twenty nations have banned the use of these seeds. For simple clarification of the issues, go to www.whfoods.com.

Fruits and vegetables

Fruits and vegetables are low-calorie carbohydrates and the storehouses of multiple nutrients. The Human Nutrition Research Center on Aging at Tufts University measured the total phytonutrient protection power of various foods. The highest-ranking vegetables include kale, broccoli, spinach and other dark greens, brussels sprouts, beets, sweet red peppers, carrots, winter squash, and tomatoes. And the best-ranking fruits are berries, oranges, pink grapefruit, apricots, plums, peaches, red grapes, and papaya. In these recipes and those you make yourself, be sure to give the above fruits and veggies top priority.

Some of the most important phytonutrients in most fruits and vegetables are antioxidants.[23] Antioxidants neutralize potentially damaging free radicals, which are known to cause chronic inflammation in body tissue.

Prepackaged backpacking meals are typically light on veggies and heavy on refined CHOs and salt. Read the packaging carefully! Backpackers need starches for energy, but I want my fruits and veggies, too, for micronutrients such as vitamins C, A, D, and E; minerals such as potassium and calcium; and beta-carotene. There are many other trace components in food that act in tandem with the few that nutritionists have scientifically isolated. This is why a vitamin or an herb supplement can never be a substitute for real food grown in rich soil. With a small amount of home preparation, you can include healthy portions of colorful, vitamin-rich fruits and vegetables in all your backpacking meals.

Treats

Sometimes we definitely need high-energy snacks. An occasional piece of candy never hurt anyone, and variety, a treat, and sense of reward are good for body and spirit, too. I get some yummy little chocolate-covered fruitcakes from a monastery,[24] and sometimes I bake up a small batch of dark chocolate brownies before the hike. Keep in mind, though, that natural sources of energy, such as dried fruits, hold the full package of vitamins, minerals, and fiber—and they are delicious. Have you ever tried dried cherries or mango or crystallized ginger or dates or black mission figs? How about sweet potato chips or a homemade granola bar with all your favorite ingredients (including dark chocolate chips)? They will give you that little nudge up the hill and staying power for hours on the trail.

Ultra foods

It has been well established in both conventional and alternative nutritional circles that some foods offer powerful ingredients that sustain and heal the body.[25] Early "health food" made most people run for cover because it put nutritional value over flavor. Thus the healthy table offered such unappetizing meals as lentil loaf and plain steamed vegetables. A few brave souls and dedicated farmers persisted, though, and now we have beautiful appetizing organic food in every grocery store, not just health food stores and farmers' markets. Chefs such as the famous Thomas Keller have even made sustainable foods a premium for gourmet cooking. And as it turns out, the most nourishing foods are completely transmutable into light, savory backpacking meals.

The palate wants more than just nourishment, though. Contemporary taste buds are global; mainstream food consumers now love Asian, Mexican, African, Caribbean, and European foods and seasonings. We want variety in our meals, and there is no turning back. The headline news is that these international dishes, as well as basic old-fashioned American meals, are made with the foods now known to be superbly healthy and healing. Every backpacker can go and go by eating meals with at least some of these fantastic ultra foods. Here are some of those foods and why they are so exceptional:

Grains

Wild or brown rice: Rice is the most popular food in the world, but the refining process robs it of 60 to 90 percent of its valuable nutrients. Unrefined varieties contain critical nutrients that rival those in fresh vegetables, such as antioxidants, minerals, vitamins, and, of course, fiber. Important for the hiker are the available niacin, calcium, magnesium, and potassium—electrolytes that relieve muscle cramps, tension, soreness, and fatigue.

Barley: Because exercise involves aerobic metabolism, it increases the production of cell-damaging molecules known as free radicals. Antioxidant micronutrients in your food scavenge for these rogues, and barley is loaded with three of the best antioxidants: selenium, copper, and tryptophan. Plus it is succulent and has a nutty flavor.

Quinoa: This ancient grain, called "the gold of the Incas," was widely honored because of its ability to increase stamina. Quinoa is a complete protein that includes all nine essential amino acids, so it is a nutritionally balanced trail food. It also has the amino acid lysine, which is essential for tissue growth and repair, useful after a hard day's scramble.

Foods to avoid: Anything white. Refined carbs cause inflammation and are devoid of essential vitamins and minerals.

Vegetables

Onion family: Onions not only give great flavor to your trail food, they are loaded with anti-inflammatory sulfur compounds, which relieve pain in muscles and joints. They also regulate blood sugar levels, which can be helpful when you've been chugging dried fruit all day to keep up your energy.

Spinach and dark leafy greens: Greens are powerhouses of vitamins and minerals, especially calcium, which enhances bone health. They also contain salicylic acid, a compound used to make aspirin. If you push it a little too hard and ache when you settle by the campfire, you'll be glad if plenty of spinach is in your hearty one-pot meal.

Yellow vegatables: Sweet potato, butternut squash, and pumpkin are filled with fiber and beta-cryptoxanthin, a pro-vitamin carotenoid. Vitamin A is important for skin and bone health as well as immune function. Fiber fills you up, balances blood sugar, and promotes good bowel health (anyone who has camped in the wild more than a day or two knows how important that is!).

Beans: One of the oldest cultivated plants in the world, beans are full of phytochemicals, such as saponins, lignans, and phytosterols, all of which offer multiple benefits. They are anti-inflammatory compounds that fight muscle damage, promote healthy brain function, protect against calcium loss, and assist in building bone mineral density. Of course, they also are loaded with fiber (so keep the tent fly open).

Foods to avoid: Prepackaged complete meals because they don't contain many veggies, and the ones in them had the life-giving nutrients processed out of them.

Fruit

Berries: These tasty delights are loaded with the antioxidant anthocyanin. Berries are as effective as aspirin at relieving muscle and joint pain after a day of endurance exercise.[26] Plus they have abundant vitamin C for a sturdy immune system. Blueberries, strawberries, raspberries, cranberries, and blackberries are delicious and easy to dehydrate and rehydrate for delicious jams, chutneys, and desserts.

Figs: Figs are high in natural and simple sugars, minerals, and fiber. They're full of potassium, magnesium, iron, copper, and manganese. Dried figs contain twice as much calcium per weight as whole milk. Calcium is important for hikers because it carries messages from your brain telling your muscles to contract, it allows your blood vessels to expand for increased blood flow, and it protects your bones when they're carrying weight and being stressed on rough terrain.

Apricots: Apricots are full of beta-carotene, dietary fiber, vitamin C, magnesium, iron, calcium, phosphorus, and potassium. Just five dried apricots give you 36 percent of the recommended daily value of vitamin A. Lycopene is a powerful antioxidant found in apricots. Include apricots in your electrolyte snack mix.

Apples: This classic fruit is so good for you that it is hard to know where to begin. We all know apples have vitamin C, but they also contain the antioxidant phloridzin, a flavanoid found only in apples. Pectin in apple skin balances cholesterol. And apples also supply boron, a little-known mineral bone protector. The quercetin in apples may protect brain cells from free radical damage. Bone and brain food: that is a ready-mixed backpacking formula!

Papaya: Papayas are luscious and are rich sources of antioxidant nutrients such as carotenes, vitamin C, and flavonoids; B vitamins such as folate and pantothenic acid; the minerals potassium and magnesium; and fiber. Together, these nutrients promote excellent cardiovascular strength. Papaya also contains the digestive enzyme papain, which is often used to treat sports injuries.

Foods to avoid: Dried fruits with sulfur or extra sugar.

Nuts

Brazil nuts: Brazil nuts are a good source of the mineral selenium, which works with proteins in the body to make antioxidant enzymes. Antioxidants help prevent cellular damage that comes from the hyper-oxidation of strenuous exercise. Brazil nuts also contain healthy fats that combat inflammation. Two Brazil nuts contain the daily recommended value of selenium. They have about fifty calories each, so just eat a few.

Almonds: Almonds are a uniquely rich superfood. They are high in monounsaturated fats, the same type of health-promoting fats found in olive oil. Almonds also have six grams of protein per ounce; and one ounce provides 50 percent of the recommended daily value of vitamin E. This tasty nut contains the minerals zinc, iron, magnesium, and potassium. Magnesium, especially, improves the flow of blood, oxygen, and nutrients throughout the body—just what you need for steady progress on the trail.

Walnuts: Walnuts are full of all the benefits of other nuts—antioxidants and minerals—but they are called "brain foods" because of their high-quality omega-3 fatty acids. Your brain is more than 60 percent structural fat and it needs omega-3s to maximize the cell's ability to usher in nutrients while eliminating wastes. This makes walnuts most valuable when you want to be clear-thinking miles away from civilization.

Tip: Soak nuts and seeds for twenty-four hours to rinse off natural enzyme inhibitors and tannins. Then dehydrate them to restore crispness.

Foods to avoid: Roasted nuts with coatings that are salty or sugary. They've often been processed in rancid oils and have unwanted additives and preservatives. If you like them a lot, check the package ingredient list carefully.

Spices[27]

Curry: Curry powders are a mixture of spices that usually include turmeric, cinnamon, cilantro (coriander), chile peppers, and ginger, all of which are proven healing foods. Each can be used separately, but by spicing your dish with curry, you get the benefit of all of them at the same time.

I like to have at least two curry-based meals per week on the trail, yet I also like variety in my meals. Each individual spice has its unique nutritional value.

Turmeric: Turmeric gives curry is golden red color. It is also an Indian remedy for digestive disorders and arthritis. What the ancients knew has been substantiated by current nutritional science. The healing micronutrient has been identified as an antioxidant called curcumin, a potent anti-inflammatory agent that soothes and repairs sore muscles and damaged cartilage. It is also effective for digestive irritation and skin rashes—both common complaints when hiking for several days.

Cilantro: Cilantro (or coriander) is high in phytonutrients, flavonoids, and polyphenols, including quercetin, a potent antioxidant that neutralizes free radicals. Quercetin also inhibits the actions of histamines and other inflammatory agents. Both Japanese and German researchers have found multiple anti-inflammatory compounds in the essential oils of cilantro.

Chile pepper: Chile pepper is a mainstay of many dishes from Mexico to Africa to Asia. The active compound in all chile peppers, from cayenne to jalapeño, is capsaicin, a well-known anti-inflammatory. Two teaspoons of chili powder provide 6 percent of the recommended daily value of vitamin C and 10 percent of vitamin A.

Ginger: Ginger is another potent antioxidant with powerful anti-inflammatory compounds called gingerols. Researchers in Denmark[28] found that the regular consumption of ginger reduces swelling and relieves pain in people with arthritis. They also observed that it improves mobility. That is the perfect remedy after a long day on the trail.

Cinnamon: Cinnamon not only improves the body's ability to utilize blood sugar, but the wonderful fragrance of this sweet spice boosts brain activity. Research found that chewing cinnamon-flavored gum, or just smelling cinnamon, enhanced cognitive processing.[29] Specifically, cinnamon improved "attentional processes," virtual recognition memory, working memory, and visual-motor speed—important tools on a hike.

Peppermint: Peppermint is an excellent source of manganese, vitamin C and vitamin A, and carotenoids, including beta-carotene. In addition to its antioxidant abilities to neutralize free radicals, rosmarinic acid in mint encourages cells to make substances that keep the airways open for easy breathing. Stop and have a cup of peppermint tea on a ridge at 12,000 feet.

Bonus food!

Dark chocolate: Did you know that dark chocolate contains eight times the number of antioxidants found in strawberries? These powerful healing polyphenols, especially the flavonoids, help lower blood pressure and fight free radical damage that results from elevated aerobic metabolism during endurance exercise. Remember that 70 percent or higher cocoa content is necessary to get the benefits.

Foods to avoid: Skip the milk chocolate and chocolate-coated candy bars, which have so much sugar that it negates the benefits of this healthy treat.

Ultra Meals for the Trail

Backpackers solve the problem of what to eat in endlessly creative ways. Some take just sugar and gorp. Think of Bill Bryson's pal hiking on the Appalachian Trail in *A Walk in the Woods*[30] who filled his pack with Twinkies. Some carry heavy canned and packaged meals along with the utensils to cook them. Imagine the Sherpas, who carry a hundred pounds or more of gear for Everest enthusiasts. Painful! Some backpackers subsist on ramen noodles and peanut butter crackers. I love to eat too much to settle for less than a real meal.

Packaged versus homemade

Dietary boredom and back-wrenching pack weight are persuasive reasons for carrying dehydrated meals, especially if you want to sustain a diet full of nourishing ultra foods with the best CHO/protein/fat/micronutrient blend. There are dozens of brands of packaged camping foods.[31] I make my meals with home-dehydrated foods. Dehydrating means drying and the words will be used interchangeably throughout the book. Here are the best reasons for doing the work yourself to make these meals at home:

Dehydrated food has excellent nutritional value. The calorie content doesn't change during hydration. It is just concentrated into a smaller mass as moisture is removed. Here is a comparison of nutritional losses in different forms of food preservation:[32]

~ Canning causes a 60 to 80 percent loss. The high loss is due to high temperatures and foods' immersion in water during period of preparation.

~ Freezing blanched food causes a 40 to 60 percent loss. Moisture expands when frozen, causing food cells to rupture.

~ Dehydrating causes a 5 to 10 percent loss. Low heat during the drying cycle and the gentle airflow result in minimal loss.

~ Fiber does not change.

~ Vitamin A is retained in dehydrated food under controlled heat methods.

~ Some thiamin, riboflavin, and niacin are lost during blanching, but if the water used to rehydrate also is consumed, you get back most of these and other minerals.

What about freeze-drying? Some hikers buy expensive freeze-dried prepackaged "healthy" and/or gourmet entrees—for some very good reasons. Freeze-dried food maintains nearly 100 percent of its nutritional value, whereas dehydrated food maintains only about 90 percent. Freeze-dried food is slightly lighter in weight, and it rehydrates faster. The texture of freeze-dried food is closer to that of the original than is dehydrated food, which tends to be a little chewy. Freeze-dried food has a longer shelf life.

There are some drawbacks, though. A freeze-drying appliance costs thousands of dollars. You can freeze-dry food in your home freezer,[33] but it takes a week to complete the process (and a lot of space), thus taking six times as long as a home dehydrator.

Even the manufacturers of "healthy" meals load their freeze-dried products with preservatives, artificial colors and flavors, and infusions of indigestible vitamins and minerals. Check the nutritional analysis, which by law they must provide on the package, and you'll find massive amounts of salt, overly processed oils (such as canola oil or trans fats), and other ingredients that are known to be unhealthy.

Many hikers like the convenience of freeze-dried entrees in which they just add boiling water to the foil pouch. But I am trying to get away from as much commercially processed food in my diet as possible. When I do eat packaged food, I follow Michael Pollan's Second Rule of Eating: "Don't eat anything with more than five ingredients, or ingredients you can't pronounce."[34] On the back of a package of freeze-dried entrees, I often see that, along with three or four "real" foods such as macaroni, onion, or tomato paste, I will be consuming disodium inosinate, potassium chloride, sugar, maltodextrin, autolyzed yeast extract, and a few other unpronounceable ingredients. My recipes, such as tasty ultra food Black-Eyed Buffalo Chili, have none of that stuff. Just real food.

There are more benefits. My desire at home and in the backcountry is to have delicious meals full of nutrition, and home dehydration is the way I make them inexpensively (about five cents per pound).[35] Dehydrating your own trail food saves buckets of money. Commercial dehydrated meals cost $4 to $8.50 per person. You also have to read the portion sizes carefully because the package might say the meal is good for two people but each serving has only +/-400 calories. Remember, you'll need about 3,000 to 4,000 calories per day to sustain energy and nutrition when backpacking, and you want those calories to be as nourishing as possible, not empty sugary fillers such as Twinkies. On the other hand, you can prepare your own dehydrated meals for less than $2 a serving and still load them with muscle building, joint-soothing, vitamin-rich tasty ultra foods.

Also, the packaging for the brand-name meals is bulky foil, which you have to pack out. Whereas you'll see in the last chapter that in your own kitchen you can pack up your meals in light baggies that crumple to almost nothing when empty, have multiple uses (I have used some as an extra water carrier), and can be washed and reused when you're back in civilization.

Plan the perfect size meals. Backpacking is not the time for fasting, and getting hungry on the trail can actually be dangerous. Low blood sugar can negatively influence decision-making skills or make you weak when you need to be alert and energetic. Many of the people who attempt and can't complete the big long-distance hikes such as the Appalachian Trail and the Continental Divide Trail fail because they take too little food, or not the right food, and become malnourished.

The trick is not carrying too much food, either. Coming home with extra pounds of rice and nuts is as ridiculous as running out of food, although not as perilous. By preparing your meals and snacks at home, you can ensure the proper proportions for your appetite and size; the right balance of protein, carbohydrates, and fats; a good number of powerfully nourishing ingredients; and the right weight for the number of days you'll be on the trail—plus a couple of emergency meals.

Dehydrated food is one quarter the portion size of what it will be when it is rehydrated. My rules of thumb for ingredient proportions in a one-pot meal for two people are:

6 to 10 slices (1 inch x 2 inches each) dehydrated meat
1/4 cup dehydrated vegetables
1/4 cup grain
1 to 4 teaspoons seasoning

Of course, some trial and error may be needed to suit your own size and metabolism, as well as the degree of difficulty of the trail. Some meals may take heavier ingredients (such as meals with foil-packed tuna), but all your meals should average about two pounds per person per day.

Simple home dehydrating techniques

The less we mess with our food, the better. The sustainable agriculture movement has taught us how close to the source we need to keep our food for sustainability as well as nutritional considerations. In fresh food the micronutrients are intact, the flavor is rich, and the textures are just right. It would be ideal to eat fresh foods on the trail, but they are too heavy because they are full of water. By taking out the water through slow heating, the weight is radically diminished. Some nutritional value is lost, but you can tell that the foods are still wholesome by their rich color, excellent flavor, and fragrant aroma. See References at the end of the book for a list of detailed dehydrating books to add to the information in *Backpackers' Ultra Food*.

Choosing a dehydrator: I use a Nesco, but there are many brands of dehydrators on the market (including Excalibur, Ronco, Mr. Coffee, Deni, and Weston), so you can choose one that is the right size and shape for your kitchen. You can also make your own solar or electric dehydrators.[36] In a pinch, you can use your oven if it can heat at 150°F or below. Some people have even used a cookie tray on the dashboard of their car for an impromptu solar dehydrator. Whatever your dehydrating tool, these basic steps will quickly demonstrate how tried and true this method of food preservation can be.

Eight steps to dehydrating

Step 1: Choose the food you are going to dry. Determine quantities based on non-dehydrated recipes (1 cup fresh food will become approximately 1/4 cup dehydrated). Check the number of servings and do the math for the size meal you want. If you walk for eight hours, you want to average about 800 to 1,000 calories per meal plus another 1,000 calories in snacks throughout the day (up to 4,000 calories).

Tip: To crank up the calories, add:

olive oil (1 tablespoon = 100 calories)
coconut oil (1 tablespoon = 120 calories)
ghee (1 tablespoon = 112 calories)
Parmesan cheese (1/4 cup grated = 113 calories)
powdered whole milk (1/2 cup = 70 calories)
raisins (1/4 cup = 100 calories)
raw sunflower seeds (1/4 cup = 190 calories)[37]

Step 2: Select similar ingredients for each round of drying so the drying temperatures and times are similar. I like to prepare veggie blends for which I dry each veggie separately and then immediately mix them together in a zip baggie. Then when I'm ready to pack up food for a trip, the veggies are ready to be assembled with other components such as protein and spices for a variety of complete meals. It is also important to manage aromas that might pass from one food to another. For example, I wouldn't dehydrate onions and raspberries in the same run. I could dehydrate onions and tomatoes together, though. Open the windows when you dry seafood. It is especially aromatic!

Step 3: Cut the food into thin slices. Berries, spinach, and peas, of course, do not need slicing. A sharp knife can make a nice thin cut (1/8 inch) in slightly frozen meat or poultry. Trim veggies into 1/4-inch slices. Thin slices dehydrate and rehydrate faster, saving energy on both ends. They also absorb marinades well and taste great.

Step 4: Pretreat some foods. A little attention goes a long way toward making dry food palatable.

~ Dunk sliced fruits in lemon juice for five minutes to prevent darkening during the drying process.

~ Use spices such as ground pepper, chili powder, curry, and teriyaki sauce in marinades for meat or poultry to tenderize and saturate them with flavors that will complement the assembled meal. I next cook the thin meat slices in a 350°F oven for 5-10 minutes, or until cooked through, before I begin to dehydrate them. This will kill any potential bacteria in the meat that can make you sick, such as salmonella and E. coli. Also, make sure to keep the meat in the refrigerator until you're ready to use it.

~ Puree sauces, including pasta sauces, as well as salsa, bean soups, and fruits for leather.

Step 5: Place the food on a dehydrator tray and set the correct temperature. Slightly separate each piece so air can circulate through the screens. This will aid in the drying process. Most dehydrators also have solid plastic trays for leathers (waxed paper works well, too). Pour purees in an even 1/4-inch layer over the tray. To make chips or crackers, pour a batter layer 1/8 inch thick.

Step 6: Dehydrate fruits and vegetables at 135°F and meat at 160°F (or according to the manufacturer's recommendations). Vegetables should be dehydrated until they are crisp, and fruits should be dehydrated until they're just slightly leathery.

Drying times will vary between five and eighteen hours. Check every few hours to see how the food is drying and estimate when it will be done. If the drying is faster on one part of the tray than another, move things around or take out the pieces that are done. If trays dry more quickly on the top or bottom position in the dryer, shift them up or down as needed.

Step 7: Store the dehydrated food in a cool, dark place. Seal it in airtight plastic bags or wide mouth canning jars. Label everything with a date. For longer shelf life, dehydrated foods can be refrigerated or frozen.

Step 8: To rehydrate dried foods, let them soak in water until they have regained their proper texture. I add purified water to the driest ingredients in a zip baggie an hour before I get to camp. This greatly reduces cooking time and saves fuel.

How to make jerky

Do not skimp on the quality of protein you purchase for making jerky. I recommend free-range lean cuts of beef, buffalo, or lamb. Always buy cage-free poultry. You can also dehydrate tuna[38] and wild salmon. When you are exercising hard, you do not want extra hormones, antibiotics, toxins, and who knows what else in your primary protein. Call a butcher and see if you can get wild game such as venison, oryx (antelope), or wild turkey. Strips of jerky make delicious snacks and fabulous one-pot soups and stews.

Tip: Vegetarians can purchase several different flavors of Spice of

Life or Primal Strips meatless vegan jerkies.

Preparation: Buy lean steaks, boneless skinless poultry, or tuna or salmon filets and freeze for a few hours. Then slice them into long, thin strips. Trim and discard all the fat, which can become rancid. If you like a chewy jerky, slice the meat with the grain into 1/4-inch strips. For a more tender, brittle jerky that is good in trail mix, slice the meat across the grain.

Marinate: Meat and poultry taste better and become tender when marinated. After marinating for 2 hours or overnight (just 30 minutes for seafood) and drying as recommended below, the jerky is ready for packaging for meals. Recipes with a seasoned jerky are prepared with the following marinades that match the flavors of the veggie blends and other seasonings. Thus red wine beef jerky is made with a jerky prepared with Red Wine Marinade, an Indian chicken jerky is jerky prepared with Indian Marinade, and so forth.

Marinades for jerky

These quantities are for 1 to 2 pounds of lean meat or poultry. You can also purchase prepared marinades for teriyaki or other flavors and follow the same general instructions below.

At Home

1. Mix all marinade or seasoning ingredients in a blender.

2. Place thin strips of meat in a shallow pan and cover with marinade.

3. Cover and refrigerate at least 2 hours or overnight (30 minutes for seafood).

HOMEMADE WORCESTERSHIRE SAUCE

Here is a healthy homemade recipe for Worcestershire sauce, which is often called for in marinades.

1/2 cup apple cider vinegar
2 tablespoons unpasteurized soy sauce

2 tablespoons water
1 tablespoon coconut sugar
1/4 teaspoon ground ginger
1/4 teaspoon ground mustard
1/4 teaspoon onion powder
1/4 teaspoon garlic powder
1/8 teaspoon ground cinnamon
1/8 teaspoon freshly ground black pepper

Combine all the ingredients in a saucepan and bring to a boil, stirring constantly. Simmer for 5 minutes, or until the sugar has dissolved. Let cool and store in the refrigerator.

BASIC MARINADE

1/4 cup unpasteurized soy sauce
1 tablespoon Homemade Worcestershire Sauce
1/2 teaspoon freshly ground black pepper
1/4 teaspoon minced garlic
1/2 teaspoon minced onion

LEMON PEPPER MARINADE

Juice from 1 large lemon
1/2 cup extra-virgin olive oil
1 teaspoon honey
1 to 2 teaspoons freshly ground black pepper
Salt to taste

INDIAN MARINADE

1 small jar tomato paste
1/2 cup extra-virgin olive oil
1/2 cup distilled white vinegar
1 to 4 tablespoons red chile flakes
1 tablespoon curry powder
1 teaspoon minced fresh ginger
1/2 teaspoon freshly ground black pepper
1/4 teaspoon minced garlic
1/2 teaspoon minced onion

Mexican Spicy Marinade

Juice from large limes
1 cup extra-virgin olive oil
2 tablespoons red chile flakes
1 teaspoon ground cumin
1 teaspoon honey
1/2 teaspoon freshly ground black pepper
1/4 teaspoon minced garlic
1/2 teaspoon minced onion

Red Wine Marinade

1 cup dry red wine
2 tablespoons Homemade Worcestershire Sauce
1/2 teaspoon ground black pepper
1/4 teaspoon minced garlic
1/2 teaspoon minced onion

Drying jerky

1. Place strips of meat, poultry, or seafood with marinade on cookie trays. Bake at 350°F for 5 to 10 minutes, or until meat is still moist but heated through.

2. Remove pan from oven, let cool, and arrange meat on dehydrator racks so the strips are close together but do not overlap. Discard excess marinade.

3. Dry at 160°F until a test piece cracks but does not break when it is bent (about 10 to 24 hours).

4. Pat off any beads of oil with absorbent toweling. Remove the meat strips from the racks and let cool.

Important tip: Seafood is strong smelling when drying so open a window or move your dehydrator out onto a porch.

Storing jerky

Package in glass jars or zip plastic baggies. Double-bag seafood to contain odor. Properly dried jerky will keep at room temperature for one to three months in a sealed container. To increase the shelf life and maintain the flavor, refrigerate or freeze the jerky.

Tip: Discard unused marinade because any bacteria from the raw meat may multiply and taint it.

How to dry fruit

Drying fruit is incredibly simple. Frozen fruit and berries dry very well. Thaw first. Use organic or wild varieties for optimum nutrition.

At Home

1. Remove skins if they are not desired. However, fruit skin has abundant nutrients because it is the part of the fruit that absorbs sunlight.
2. Slice fruit into uniform 1/4- to 3/8-inch-thick pieces.
3. To preserve fruit color, soak the slices for 3 to 5 minutes in a solution made with the juice of one to four lemons per quart of water. Remove the slices and lightly pat dry.
4. Dehydrate at 135°F until the slices are leathery but not brittle, from 6 to 20 hours depending on the fruit. Wetter fruits such as grapes, plums, and cherries take the most time.

Tip: Boil cranberries for 2 minutes to pop the skins before drying.

Tip: All dehydrated fruits mentioned in the recipes are dried at home.

How to make leathers

Leathers are made from any pureed individual fruit or fruit blends. They are as delicious as regular dehydrated fruit, although the texture is different. Leathers can be flavored or sweetened. I love to have a variety of fruit leathers because they can be added to dried fruit to thicken sauces and chutney. They also add variety to my snack bag. Here are two recipes for delicious fruit leather condiments.

At Home

1. Blend fresh or frozen fruit into a puree. Do not add water. It should have about the same consistency as thin applesauce.
2. Spread the puree evenly about 1/4 inch thick on a solid dehydrator tray.
3. Dehydrate the puree at 135°F until it is leathery but not brittle, from 6 to 20 hours depending on the fruit. Wetter fruits take the most time.
4. Roll the leather and pack in zip baggies.

INDIAN CHUTNEY LEATHER

1 cup sliced fresh mango
1 cup sliced fresh papaya
1/2 teaspoon allspice
1/2 teaspoon ground cinnamon
1/2 teaspoon ground nutmeg
1/4 teaspoon chili powder
1/2 cup raisins
1/2 cup hot water

At Home

1. Puree all the ingredients except the raisins and water.
2. Spread the puree 1/4 inch thick on a dehydrating tray.
3. Dry at 135°F until it is leathery but not brittle.
4. Roll the leather and pack it in zip baggies along with the raisins.

In Camp

Pour the 1/2 cup hot water over the raisins and the leather. Add more water as needed for a sauce-like consistency.

CRAN-RASP-BLACKBERRY MINT SAUCE LEATHER

1/2 cup fresh or frozen cranberries

1/2 cup fresh or frozen blackberries
1/2 cup fresh or frozen raspberries
1/4 cup minced fresh mint leaves
1/2 cup dried cranberries
1/2 cup hot water as needed for consistency

At Home

1. Thaw the berries if needed and blend them with the mint until they are pureed.
2. Spread the puree 1/4 inch thick on a dehydrating tray.
3. Dehydrate at 135°F until the puree is leathery but not brittle.
4. Roll and pack in a zip baggie along with the dried cranberries.

In Camp

1. Tear leather into small pieces.
2. Pour the 1/2 cup hot water over the dried cranberries and the leather (either in the zip baggie or a cup).
3. Stir and add more water as needed to achieve the texture of a sauce with some whole cranberries.

TOMATO SAUCE LEATHER

At Home

1. Prepare or purchase your favorite tomato sauce and puree the sauce in a blender.
2. Spread the sauce 1/4 inch thick on a dehydrating tray.
3. Dry at 135°F until the sauce is leathery but not brittle.
4. Roll the leather and pack in a zip baggie.

In Camp

1. Tear leather into small pieces.
2. Pour 1/2 cup hot water over the leather in a cup or baggie.
3. Stir and add more water as needed to achieve a sauce-like texture.

Salsa Leather

At Home

1. Prepare or purchase your favorite salsa and puree the salsa in a blender.
2. Spread the salsa 1/4 inch thick on a dehydrating tray.
3. Dry at 135°F until the salsa is leathery but not brittle.
4. Roll the leather and pack it in a zip baggie.

In Camp

1. Tear leather into small pieces.
2. Pour 1/2 cup hot water over the leather in a cup or baggie.
3. Stir and add more water as needed to achieve a salsa-like texture.

Tip: If you like a chunky salsa, soak dehydrated onion, garlic, jalapeño, and tomatoes until soft and then add to the rehydrated leather with an extra 1/4 cup water. Cook for 5 minutes, or until soft.

Soup Bark

Any pureed soup can be made into "bark" and reconstituted. This is especially good for pea soup and bean soups, which normally take a long time to cook.

At Home

1. Puree 4 cups of your favorite cooked pea or bean soup in a blender.
2. Spread the puree 1/4 inch thick on a dehydrator tray.
3. Dehydrate the puree until it is brittle enough to break into ragged pieces, called "bark."
4. Divide into two equal portions and store in two zip baggies.

In Camp

1. Add 2 cups water to one zip baggie of soup bark.
2. Rehydrate and cook, adding choice of extra soaked veggies and jerky as needed for texture and flavor.

How to dehydrate grains

Cook rice, barley, quinoa, or other grain as usual. I find a brown, red, and wild rice mixture especially flavorful and nourishing. Spread the cooked grain on a dehydrating tray and dry it at 135°F until it is crisp. The camp cooking time for dehydrated grains will be reduced by half, although it is reduced by half again if you soak the grains for at least an hour before the final cooking in camp.

Tip: All dehydrated grains mentioned in the recipes are dehydrated at home.

How to cook trail pasta

Many pastas (which are already dehydrated) require up to 12 minutes of boiling to cook all the way through. A quicker process is to soak in cold water, and in 15 to 45 minutes (thicker pasta like fettuccini takes longer than thin varieties like capellini), it will become cold rehydrated pasta, soft and ready to use. Hot or warm water will speed up the rehydration. I add the softened pasta to the warm sauce for 1 to 5 minutes and have a great hot pasta dish.

How to prepare veggies and veggie blends

At Home

1. Slice vegetables uniformly into 1/4-inch x 1/4-inch pieces. The smaller the piece, the quicker the dehydrating and rehydrating.
2. Dry them at 135°F until they are crisp.
3. Package the veggie blends in zip baggies.

Tip: I also dry and package about six onions for a crunchy topping on any dish. Some recipes also call for extra veggies like potatoes or spinach. All dehydrated veggies mentioned in the recipes are dried at home.

INDIAN VEGGIE BLEND

1 onion
4 to 6 cloves garlic
1 eggplant
8 ounces fresh mushrooms
1 pound fresh spinach
1/2 cup fresh or frozen peas

MEXICAN SPICY VEGGIE BLEND

1 onion
4 to 6 cloves garlic
2 red or green sweet bell peppers
2 to 4 hot chile peppers (jalapeño, cayenne, chipotle, habanero, et cetera)
6 to 8 fresh or canned Roma tomatoes
1/2 bunch fresh cilantro

BASIC VEGGIE STEW BLEND

2 potatoes
1 parsnip
8 ounces fresh mushrooms
1 carrot
1 onion
4 to 6 cloves garlic
1/2 bunch fresh parsley
1 pound fresh spinach
1/2 cup fresh or frozen peas

ASIAN VEGGIE BLEND

1 onion
2 to 4 cloves garlic
1/2 cup chopped cabbage
1/2 pound fresh spinach

ITALIAN VEGGIE BLEND

1 onion
2 to 4 cloves garlic

2 zucchini
6 to 8 fresh or canned Roma tomatoes
1/2 bunch fresh parsley

How to make crackers

Crackers make perfect lunch food or a side with a dinner soup. Flax seeds are a fine base because they become gelatinous when soaked. Flax is also one of the plant foods highest in omega-3 fatty acids, which lubricate your joints.

CAJUN FLAX ALMOND CRACKERS

1/2 cup raw almonds
1 cup flax seeds
1/4 cup sunflower seeds
1/2 cup sesame seeds
2 carrots
1/4 red onion
1 clove garlic
1/2 cup Italian parsley
2 fresh or canned Roma tomatoes
2 cups fresh spinach
1 teaspoon freshly squeezed lemon juice
1 tablespoon Cajun seasoning
Salt or soy sauce to taste

1. Soak the nuts and seeds in water for a few hours. You'll know that they're ready to go when the flax seeds become gelatinous.

2. Strain, chop, and blend all the soaked nuts and seeds.

3. Puree the veggies and transfer to a large bowl. Add the prepared nuts and seeds, lemon juice, and Cajun seasoning; mix well. Add the salt or soy sauce and stir to combine.

4. Spread the mixture onto two dehydrator trays, 1/8 inch thick for chips or 1/4 inch thick for crackers. You can experiment with the thickness.

5. Dry at 105°F overnight. In the morning, flip them over and dry for another 4 to 5 hours.

Southwest Flax Crackers

1/2 cup raw sunflower seeds
1/2 cup julienned dried tomatoes
1/2 cup flax seed
2 cloves garlic, pressed
1 small jalapeño, seeded and minced
1/4 cup fresh cilantro
1 tablespoon red chile flakes
1 tablespoon olive oil
1 teaspoon sea salt

At Home

1. Grind the sunflower seeds into meal (a coffee grinder works well).

2. Soak the dried tomatoes for at least 1 hour in just enough water to cover them.

3. Soak the flax seed for at least 2 hours in just enough water to keep them from clumping.

4. Transfer the tomatoes and soaking water to a blender. Add the garlic, jalapeño, cilantro, chili, and olive oil. Blend into a chunky paste. Transfer the paste into a bowl and stir in the soaked flax seed, ground sunflower seed, and sea salt.

5. Spread on dehydrator sheets and dehydrate for 3 to 4 hours at 105°F.

6. Using a knife, carefully cut into squares. Continue to dry for 6 more hours.

7. Flip the crackers and dry until they're crisp, about 18 hours total drying time.

Sunflower Flax Chips

These are between a cracker and a chip, good with tuna or nut butter or hummus for lunch.

2 cups sunflower seeds, soaked for 4 to 6 hours and then drained
1 large onion, chopped
1 clove garlic, minced

58

2 cups flax seeds, soaked in 1 1/3 cups water for 4 to 6 hours and
then drained
1 tablespoon dried basil
1 tablespoon dried thyme
1 tablespoon dried oregano
1/4 cup soy sauce
Sea salt and ground black pepper to taste

At Home

1. Place the drained sunflower seeds, the onion, and the garlic
in a blender. Add a little water if necessary and blend to combine.
2. Transfer to a large bowl and add the drained flax seeds, herbs,
soy sauce, salt, and pepper. Mix well.
3. Spread the mixture 1/4 inch thick onto dehydrator trays (or
waxed paper) and dry at 105°F for 6 hours. Flip and dry for 6
more hours.
4. Break into pieces and store in zip baggies.

Tip: If you spread the cracker or chip batter too thin when dehydrating, the pieces can be quite brittle and/or crumbly. Experiment
with the thickness.

CHEESE CRISPS

There is nothing like cheese to add the final touch of flavor to a
one-pot meal, and crisps are the simplest and lightest way to carry
cheese into the backcountry. You can sprinkle these crisps over the
dish as a crispy topping. Or you can make a cream sauce with powdered milk, ghee, and Cheese Crisps. A dry, hard cheese such as
Parmesan or Asiago works best, but experiment with different kinds.

At Home

1. Grate the cheese and sprinkle it uniformly on a dehydrator tray.
2. Dry the cheese at 140°F for 4 to 6 hours, or until brittle. If the
cheese becomes oily, pat it dry with a paper towel and continue
dehydrating.

3. Crumble it into pieces and store in zip baggies.

Tip: Grated cheese can be seasoned before drying to make a tasty snack. Use garlic powder, chili powder, ground black pepper, or Cajun seasoning.

Backpackers' Pantry

Some seasonings will already have been added to your veggie blends. At home, put any extra seasonings into the smallest zip baggies you can find, such as those for bulk spices at a health food store. You can include any or all of the following for a seven-day trip; quantities depend on how much weight you want to carry.

Optional herbs and spices

Sea salt or Himalayan salt (essential for electrolytes)
Ground black pepper
Curry powder
Red chile flakes
Italian seasoning blend (1 teaspoon each dried oregano, thyme, basil, parsley)
Cajun seasoning blend (1/2 teaspoon each paprika, black pepper, cayenne, dried garlic, oregano, thyme)
Mexican seasoning blend (1/2 teaspoon each cayenne, cumin, dried cilantro, dried garlic)
Turkish seasoning blend (1/4 teaspoon each ground cinnamon, ground cardamom, ground nutmeg, chopped dried mint, and ground cloves)
Dry mustard
Garlic powder
Dried mint

Dehydrated lemon zest
Vegetable or beef bouillon cubes
Soy sauce or tamari in individual packets

Optional packaged foods

Miso soup
Tabouli
Hummus
Rice noodles
Linguini, capellini, or thin spaghetti
Couscous
Powdered whole milk: For the richest flavor, I like Backpacker's
Pantry whole milk powder found at REI
Nori seaweed, for wraps or Asian soups
Bean soup mix
Parmesan cheese
Foil-packed tuna or salmon

Optional sweeteners

Coconut sugar
Raw sugar
Honey in individual packets
Other artificial sweeteners

Tip: Research the latest information on alternative sweeteners. Opinions vary and change as these are incorporated into mainstream diets.

Optional cooking oils

Olive oil: 1 tablespoon per day per person plus a 1/4 cup each for pesto, hummus, and/or tabouli
Coconut oil: 1 tablespoon per day to be added to one-pot meals
Ghee: Ghee is a South Asian clarified butter that does not need to be refrigerated because it has been cooked to remove all milk solids and water. The milk solids are browned in the fat and then strained

out. This gives ghee a rich, nutty flavor; it is delicious on breakfast cereals, grains, and desserts. Take at least 1 tablespoon per person per day. Ghee can be purchased at local markets such as Whole Foods, various natural grocery stores, or grocery cooperatives. Or you can make it at home with this recipe.

GHEE

It takes time, patience, and attention to make ghee, so I recommend processing at least 2 to 4 pounds of butter at once. Note that 1 pound of butter makes about 1 1/2 cups ghee.

Pure unsalted butter (not margarine!)

At Home

1. Heat the butter in a saucepan or a double boiler over medium heat until it bubbles. Do not cover the pan.

2. Reduce the heat to low and simmer about 30 minutes, uncovered, or until the butter turns a clear golden color. Do not let it burn!

3. Skim off the foam solids that appear on the surface. When the ghee is clear, carefully pour it into another pan, leaving the milk solids on the bottom of the first pot.

4. Simmer the clear liquid again to boil off any final water. Let cool while the remaining solids settle out.

5. Pour the ghee into containers through cheesecloth or a coffee filter.

6. Store it in a sealed plastic container or double-bagged with zip baggies. Use ghee in all your regular cooking.

Remember: Ghee does not have to be refrigerated.

Trail Snacks

R emember to STOP! EAT! DRINK! REST! at regular intervals on long hikes. Your snacks[39] can make the difference between a fun, safe journey and a slog.

Electrolyte-rich trail snacks

Make a mixture that includes some of these ingredients to get the essentials for electrolyte replacement.

Sodium

Seaweed (such as dulse)
Hard cheese
High mineral sea or Himalayan salt (season your dehydrated chips and add a tiny pinch to your water bottle)

Potassium

Citrus (add dehydrated lime, lemon, or orange slices to your water)
Shredded coconut and/or coconut sugar
Banana chips
Kale chips
Sweet potato chips

Calcium

Hard cheese with whole-grain cracker
Almonds

Sesame seeds or sesame butter (tahini)
Apricots

Magnesium chloride

Salmon jerky
Mixed nuts, such as almonds, walnuts, pecans, and cashews
Edamame or soy nuts
Peanut butter
Whole-grain crackers

ULTRA TRAIL MIX

On hikes lasting several days, I get tired of the same old snack mix. I like my gorp to have a variety of chunky energy foods so I can poke around for the one thing that strikes my fancy. Perhaps it is a piece of mango, a couple of chocolate chips, or a Brazil nut. Here is a trail mix of ultra foods for ultra energy and ultra variety.

1/2 cup dark chocolate chips
2 cups combined dried fruit, such as cherries, mango, papaya, apricots, pineapple, and figs
1/2 cup large Flame raisins
2 cups combined raw nuts, such as walnuts, almonds, cashews, Brazil nuts, hazelnuts, peanuts, and/or pine nuts
1/2 cup sunflower seeds
1/2 cup pumpkin seeds

Granola Bars

When you're bored with trail mix, the crunch of a granola bar can be very satisfying. Did you know that chewing crisp food triggers a mild endorphin release?[40] Endorphins are neurochemicals that soothe aches and pains.

SIMPLE CRUNCHY GRANOLA BAR

4 cups of your favorite dry granola (Or make your own!)
1/2 cup coconut sugar
3/4 cup butter, melted

1/2 cup honey
1 teaspoon vanilla extract
1/4 teaspoon ground cinnamon
1 teaspoon salt

At Home

1. Combine all the ingredients and mix well.
2. Press into well-greased cookie sheet.
3. Bake for 10 to 12 minutes at 450°F.
4. Let cool and cut into bars.
5. Pack in zip baggies.

Brand-name protein bars

There is a great variety of trail bars, and each offers something different in flavor and nutritional analysis. Brands include Clif, PowerBar, Larabar, Odwalla, Honey Stinger, and ProBar. Each brand has several varieties, including some with extra protein. I sometimes take along the Clif Mojo because it has a lot of big pieces of unprocessed nuts and crunchy pretzels. My other choices are the raw food Pro Bar and the high-cal Stinger Bar. My tastes change. The point is to experiment with what suites you in terms of flavor, calories, nutrient balance, and texture. Be sure to check on the weight, too, because you don't necessarily want to pack in a few pounds of power bars (and pack out the wrappers).

Drinks

Water, water, water: Drink 3 to 6 quarts a day depending on exertion and temperature. Add a tiny pinch of salt and dry citrus for electrolytes. Or carry packets of powdered electrolytes such as Emergen-C.

Coffee: I haven't found a trail coffee-making system that results in a truly rich brew. Powdered coffee tends to be bitter or flavorless. Drip coffee usually ends up being cold by the time it fills the mug.

French press seems too urbane for the trail and would probably also be cold by the time it reached my mug. But I do like my caffeine, so first thing in the morning I drink a tasty mocha.

MOCHA MIX

This recipe makes enough mocha mix for five mornings.

8 tablespoons dark chocolate powder
4 tablespoons coconut sugar
8 tablespoons whole milk powder
8 to 10 tablespoons powdered espresso, or 8 to 10 packets Starbucks instant dark roast coffee

At Home

1. Mix the chocolate, sugar, and milk powder and seal it in a quart zip baggie.

2. Seal the espresso powder or coffee packets in a zip snack baggie.

In Camp

1. Spoon 4 tablespoons mocha mix into a mug.

2. Add 1 to 2 tablespoons espresso powder or packets of coffee as desired.

3. Add 2 to 4 tablespoons water (hot water will prevent lumps) and stir to combine.

4. Add 1 1/2 cups hot water and stir well.

Tip: Some hikers prefer to brew ground coffee in a lightweight aluminum percolator. Apparently the higher the altitude, the better the brew. Liquid coffee concentrates are also available.

Herb teas: Ginger, mint, and Bengal spice aid digestion. I also drink a cup of bedtime blend with chamomile and valerian after dinner. It helps keep minor aches and pains from waking me up.

Black tea: There is nothing better than a cup of black tea (Earl Grey, Darjeeling, Assam, English Breakfast, or Irish Breakfast) to wake you up in the morning and/or give you a boost in the afternoon. Black tea is a great source of antioxidants to replenish your stiff limbs and/or sore muscles. Make it more delicious with whole milk powder and a sweetener of choice (mix the powder with a bit of hot water first to avoid clumping). I love looking forward to midafternoon on the hike when I get a cup of tea and, if I'm very good, a cookie.

Green, white, and red teas: These recently popular teas have the same healing polyphenols as black tea. They are not all to my taste, but I know they have the similar reviving power of a black tea.

Instant drink options: Instant apple cider mix, Emergen-C (for vitamins, minerals, and electrolytes), lemonade powder.

Backcountry Breakfasts

I often get up at dawn to make some distance before afternoon rains. I eat a quick snack (a granola bar or an energy bar) with my mocha and then pack up. I eat a hot breakfast a couple of hours later when it is light and I've covered some ground. Here are good hot breakfasts that really fill me up along with a second mocha or tea. For those who like to take a little longer in morning camp, these breakfasts offer a filling wakeup. All of these recipes[41] serve one person.

HOT SPROUTED BUCKWHEAT MUESLI

This mix has the double textures of crunchy sprouted buckwheat and hot soft muesli. The mix can be sweetened more by adding extra dried fruit. For more protein, add extra nuts. The muesli can also be eaten cold.

> 1/4 cup raw buckwheat groats
> 1/4 cup 1-minute rolled oats
> 10 raisins
> 10 dried berries
> 1/8 cup slivered almonds or other nuts
> 2 tablespoons powdered whole milk
> 1/4 teaspoon ground cinnamon
> 3/4 cup hot water
> Sweetener as needed

At Home

1. Soak the buckwheat in water overnight, and then sprout it in a jar or a sprouter.
2. Dehydrate the sprouted buckwheat for 3 to 6 hours. Let cool and then store in a zip baggie.
3. Mix all the other dry ingredients and store in a zip baggie.

In Camp

Add the 3/4 cup hot water to the dry ingredients and stir well. Let it sit a minute or two, and then top with the crunchy buckwheat and the sweetener. Enjoy!

INSTANT GRITS WITH NUTS, DRIED FRUIT, AND GHEE

The word *grits* comes from the Old English "greot," meaning something ground. Grits are a ground corn product common in southern cooking. The alkaline soaking process used to process grits releases the corn's niacin and lysine.

1 packet instant grits, or 1/2 cup dehydrated cooked grits from home
1/4 cup mixed chopped nuts and dried fruit
2 tablespoons powdered whole milk
1 teaspoon ghee

Add all the ingredients to a bowl and pour on hot water as per packet instructions.

HOT RICE PUDDING

This is a great breakfast the morning after a dinner with rice. Cook up an extra 1/4 cup rice per person and leave it in a baggie in your bear bag overnight (unless you are camping in a hot climate, in which case cook the rice in the morning).

1/2 cup water
1/4 cup leftover cooked rice

2 tablespoons whole milk powder
1 tablespoon sunflower seeds
1 teaspoon sweetener (or just sweeten the pudding with extra dried fruit)
1 teaspoon ghee
1/4 teaspoon ground cinnamon
1/4 teaspoon ground nutmeg
1/8 teaspoon salt
Nuts to taste sprinkled on top

In Camp
1. Boil the 1/2 cup water. Add the rice, milk powder, seeds, and sweetener.
2. Turn off the heat and let sit for 5 minutes.
3. Add the ghee and sprinkle with the cinnamon, nutmeg, and salt. Sprinkle nuts to taste on top.

BREAKFAST OAT-NUT COOKIE

Bake these nourishing treats at home and freeze them until you are ready to hit the trail. They are a filling breakfast for an early morning start and energizing with your afternoon tea, too. This recipe makes about 2 dozen cookies.

1/3 cup granola
1/2 cup orange juice
3/4 cup butter, softened
1/4 cup coconut sugar
1 egg
1/4 cup honey
1 1/2 teaspoons vanilla extract
1 cup plus 1 to 2 teaspoons unbleached organic flour or your pre-ferred gluten-free flour
1 teaspoon baking powder
1/2 teaspoon baking soda
1/2 teaspoon salt
1/3 cup powdered milk
2 teaspoons grated orange zest

1 cup plus 1 to 2 teaspoons regular rolled oats
1 cup chopped nuts
1 cup raisins or currants

At Home

1. Combine the granola and juice in a large bowl and let stand.

2. In a medium bowl, cream the butter, sugar, egg, honey, and vanilla.

3. Add the butter mixture to the granola mixture and blend well.

4. In a medium bowl combine the flour, baking powder, baking soda, and salt. Add the powdered milk and stir to combine, then add to the granola mixture.

5. Add the orange zest, oats, nuts, and raisins. Mix well. Add a little flour if the dough is too sticky.

6. Drop the dough by teaspoonfuls onto a lightly greased cookie sheet. Bake at 375°F for 10 to 12 minutes, or until golden brown.

SUNFLOWER SEED PANCAKE FRUIT JAM WRAP

Makes 2 pancakes

FRUIT JAM

1 or 2 rolls fruit leather
1/2 cup hot water
1 teaspoon ground cinnamon

In Camp

1. Place the fruit leather in a zip baggie and add the 1/2 cup hot water and the cinnamon. Add other chunks of dried fruit as desired for a chunky texture.

2. Let the leather soak, and stir it occasionally as the leather turns to jam.

PANCAKE BATTER MIX

1 cup flour of choice

1 to 2 tablespoons sunflower seeds
Baking powder as needed per elevation (below)
1 teaspoon ground cinnamon
1/4 teaspoon salt (optional)
1/4 to 1/3 cup powdered whole milk
1 cup water
2 to 4 tablespoons ghee or coconut oil
Fruit Jam

At Home

Place the flour, sunflower seeds, baking powder, cinnamon, and
salt in a zip baggie and label it.

In Camp

1. Mix the bagged dry ingredients with the powdered milk and
water until the batter easily runs off a spoon.

2. Warm the ghee or oil in a large skillet over medium heat; spoon
in a thin layer of the batter.

3. When bubbles cover the surface of the pancake, flip it and
cook the second side.

4. Wrap the pancake around a generous spoonful of Fruit Jam.

Note: Altitude and double-acting baking powder
0–3,500 feet: Use 2 teaspoons per cup of flour.
3,500–6,500 feet: Use 1 3/4 teaspoons per cup of flour.
6,500–8,500 feet: Use 1 1/2 teaspoons per cup of flour.
8,500–10,000 feet: Use 1 1/4 teaspoons per cup of flour.
Over 10,000 feet: Use 1 teaspoon baking powder plus 1 tablespoon
powdered egg per cup of flour.

WARM PUMPKIN GRANOLA CRISP

1 can (15 ounces) pumpkin or 1 1/2 cups home-baked pumpkin
1/2 teaspoon each ground nutmeg, ground cinnamon, and allspice
Honey, raw sugar, coconut sugar, or other sweetener as needed
1/4 to 1/2 cup water

1 homemade crispy granola bar

At Home

1. Season the pureed pumpkin with the ground spices.
2. Add sweetener to taste and blend well.
3. Spread the pumpkin puree on a dehydrator tray and dry at 135°F until it is leathery.
4. Let cool, roll the leather, and package in zip baggies.

In Camp

1. Boil the 1/4 to 1/2 cup water. Place 1 or 2 rolls of the pumpkin leather in a zip baggie. Add the water and let the leather soak, stirring occasionally as the leather turns to sauce.
2. Break up the granola bar into bits in the bottom of a bowl.
3. Pour the warm pumpkin sauce over the granola bits and serve.

HOT APPLE ALMOND QUINOA CEREAL

1/2 cup dehydrated quinoa
1 cup water
2 tablespoons chopped almonds
1 tablespoon raisins
2 tablespoons chopped dried apples
2 tablespoons powdered whole milk
1/2 teaspoon ground cinnamon
1 teaspoon coconut sugar (optional)

At Home

1. Cook the quinoa according to package instructions.
2. Dehydrate for 2 to 6 hours, and package 1/2 cup per zip baggie.

In Camp

Boil the 1 cup water. Add the dehydrated quinoa and the remaining ingredients, stir well, and simmer for 10 minutes, or until soft and thick.

Backcountry Lunches

A hearty lunch[42] is a must. I'm always famished because I've usu-ally already walked four hours by midday. I like a meal that is thoroughly filling but not too troublesome to assemble. Instead of cooking at lunch, I save my fuel for a reviving afternoon tea. The quantities below are based on servings for one person for three days.

Fresh trail veggies

These durable nutritious veggies keep for two to three days (de-pending on outdoor temperatures). I pack them next to the water bladder inside my pack to keep them as cool as possible. I like the crunch and the fiber.

    1 sandwich bag of sunflower sprouts
    1 sandwich bag of parsley sprigs
    4 to 6 radishes – a crunchy cruciferous veggie with lots of support
    for muscles and cartilage
    4 to 6 baby carrots – full of beta-carotene
    1 red bell pepper, sliced – great-tasting vitamin C

Perishable foods

Use up your perishable food during the first few days. Remember to weigh everything. Then weigh the value of these foods against the strength of your back, shoulders, and thighs and the degree of difficulty of the trail.

> 2 to 4 tortillas or pita bread
> 1 fresh apple or orange
> 4 ounces hard artisanal cheese, such as Parmesan or Asiago
> 1 small hard sausage

Nonperishable lunch foods

Lunches need variety and a core of nonperishable items that you can count on when the veggies and perishables are gone.

> 8 ounces crackers
> 2 packages (1 1/2 ounces each) nut butter (bulk can be packaged in snack size zip baggies, or use prepackaged brands such as Justin's or Artisana Organic)
> 1 to 4 foil packs tuna (3 ounces each)
> 1 package instant tabouli, divided into two portions (you will need 1 tablespoon olive oil for each)
> 2 packets miso soup
> Nori seaweed sheets, to make wraps

Hummus

Hummus is a dip/spread that is made from chickpeas (or garbanzo beans in Spanish). It is one of the oldest foods, dating back over 7,000 years ago. It is a great lunch for backpackers because these legumes contain both carbohydrates and protein. Two tablespoons of hummus has about fifty calories. There are several brands of instant hummus, but you can make your own dehydrated hummus at home. Start with canned chickpeas, or cook dried chickpeas from scratch.

Basic Homemade Dehydrated Hummus

> 4 cloves garlic, minced and then mashed
> 2 cups cooked or canned chickpeas

1/3 cup freshly squeezed lemon juice
1/2 teaspoon sea salt or to taste
1/4 cup olive oil (to be added on the trail or in camp)

At Home

1. In a food processor or blender, combine the garlic, chickpeas, and lemon juice. Process until smooth. Add the sea salt to taste.
2. Spread the hummus onto a solid food dehydrator tray. Dry until the hummus is crisp, usually overnight.
3. Grind the dry hummus to a powder. Separate the powder into two portions and pour into two zip baggies. Each baggie will provide enough hummus for two people.

For variations, consider flavoring the original recipe with sun-dried tomatoes, roasted eggplant, steamed spinach, and/or roasted red bell pepper. For higher fat and protein content, add ground walnuts or hazelnuts, tahini (roasted ground sesame seeds), and/or pine nuts.

On the Trail

One hour before lunch, start the rehydration. Add 1/8 cup olive oil and about 1/2 cup water to each bag to thoroughly soak the powder. Check the consistency of the rehydrating hummus and add more water if needed to get a creamy, spreadable consistency.

Lunch menu for seven days

Plan your lunches according to perishable ingredients and their weight. Also, think about what dinner you can eat that will make use of the perishables. On a long hike, resupply fresh foods after several days.

Day 1: Tuna with sprouts and red bell pepper strips on pita, tortilla, or crackers (dinner: pita or tortilla with soup)

Day 2: Hummus with sprouts and red bell pepper on pita, tortilla, or crackers (dinner: pita or tortilla with Split Pea Soup)

Day 3: Asiago cheese and flax crackers with radish and carrot (dinner: fusilli pasta with Asiago sauce)

Day 4: Tabouli wrapped in nori with radish and carrot

Day 5: Nut butter on sunflower crackers

Day 6: Sun-dried tomato hummus wrapped in nori

Day 7: Hard sausage and almond crackers

Backcountry Dinners

These sample meals offer a variety of taste combinations, and the ingredients are built from the dehydrated foods and food blends that you have prepared at home. They also make use of some of the packaged foods in the Backpackers' Pantry. I hope these ideas inspire you to take any recipe[43] from any cookbook and make your own backpackers' ultra food meals.

Bean dishes

MEXICAN BEAN SOUP WITH RICE AND SPICY BEEF

Spicy Mexican food tastes so good around a campfire or when it is cold or rainy. This is also a good meal for the first night on the trail because you can serve it with fresh tortillas and cheese. Rehydrate some Salsa Leather in 1/2 cup warm water and add a dollop on your tortilla or in your soup for an extra boost of flavor. Also, by eliminating the rice and using less water, the beans and veggies make a great burrito spread.

1/4 cup Mexican spicy beef jerky
1/4 cup dehydrated rice blend
1/2 cup Mexican Spicy Veggie Blend
1/2 package black bean soup mix, or 1 zip baggie of homemade

bean soup bark
1 or 2 rolls Salsa Leather
3 cups water
A pinch of dehydrated onion

In Camp

1. Presoak the beef jerky, rice, and veggies together for 1 hour before cooking.
2. Prepare the black bean soup mix per package instructions. Or rehydrate the black bean soup bark.
3. Rehydrate the Salsa Leather in 1 cup of the water.
4. Add the presoaked rice, beef, and veggies and simmer in the remaining 2 cups water for 10 minutes.
5. If the rice and beef are still crunchy, let them sit for 10 minutes and then reheat briefly.
6. Serve with tortillas, rehydrated Salsa Leather, and dehydrated onion on top.

MIDDLE EASTERN RED LENTILS WITH TURKEY

Red lentils cook in half the time it takes for green or brown lentils.

1/3 cup dehydrated red lentils
1 cup dehydrated Indian Veggie Blend
1/2 cup Indian turkey jerky
1 teaspoon Turkish seasoning blend
1 or 2 rolls Tomato Sauce Leather
3 to 4 cups water
1 tablespoon olive oil
1 tablespoon coarsely chopped cashews, for garnish

At Home

1. Precook the lentils and dehydrate for 4 to 6 hours.
2. Add Turkish seasoning blend and package in a zip baggie.

In Camp

1. Presoak the dehydrated seasoned lentils, Indian Veggie Blend, and turkey jerky together for 1 hour before cooking.

2. Over low heat, rehydrate the Tomato Sauce Leather in the water and the olive oil, stirring slowly and adding water as needed until the leather is fully reconstituted.

3. Add the lentil mixture and cook for 10 to 15 minutes, or until soft.

4. If the lentils are still a little crunchy, let them sit for 10 minutes and then reheat briefly.

5. Serve in two bowls. Sprinkle each with the chopped cashews.

BLACK-EYED BUFFALO CHILI

Prepare the Mexican Spicy Veggie Blend to your desired level of heat. I like my chili really hot—TexMex-style—so I add extra red chile flakes during cooking. Dried tomatoes add great texture when cooked with Tomato Sauce Leather. This chili goes well with Southwest Flax Crackers.

1/2 cup dehydrated black-eyed peas
1/2 cup spicy buffalo jerky
1/2 cup Mexican Spicy Veggie Blend
3 to 4 cups water
1 or 2 rolls Tomato Sauce Leather
1/4 cup dried tomatoes
Extra red chile flakes to taste
1/2 cup Cheddar Cheese Crisps

1. Presoak the black-eyed peas, buffalo jerky, and veggie blend 1 hour before cooking.

2. Boil the 3 to 4 cups water. Add the presoaked peas, buffalo, and veggie blend, and the Tomato Sauce Leather, sun-dried tomatoes, and extra red chile flakes. Reduce the heat to medium and cook for 15 minutes.

3. Serve in two bowls and sprinkle each with Cheddar Cheese Crisps.

CUBAN BLACK BEANS WITH RICE

Cuban beans are a mixture of spicy and sweet.

1/2 cup dehydrated black beans
1/2 cup dehydrated rice blend
1 package Mexican Spicy Veggie Blend
3 to 4 cups water
1 roll Salsa Leather
1 teaspoon coconut sugar
Extra red chile flakes as needed
Ground black pepper to taste
1 teaspoon dehydrated onion
1 teaspoon Cheese Crisps

In Camp

1. Presoak the beans, rice, and veggies 1 hour before cooking.

2. Bring the 3 to 4 cups water to a boil and add the Salsa Leather, veggie mixture, sugar, red chile flakes, and ground pepper.

3. Cook for 10 to 15 minutes. If the beans are still crunchy, let them sit an extra 10 minutes and then briefly reheat.

4. Serve with a topping of dehydrated onion and Cheese Crisps.

Grain and rice dishes

BLACK RICE CURRY WITH TURKEY AND CHUTNEY

Black rice blends are absolutely delicious. By precooking and drying them, even the wild rice will cook quickly and absorb all the other flavors in the dish.

1 roll chutney leather
1/4 cup dehydrated black rice blend
6 to 8 pieces Indian turkey jerky
1/4 cup Indian Veggie Blend
3 1/2 cups water
6 to 12 raisins or to taste
1 teaspoon extra curry powder or red chile flakes (optional)

At Home

1. Make a chutney leather with your favorite chutney recipe or the chutney recipe on page 52.
2. Cook and dehydrate the black rice blend.

In Camp

1. Presoak the rice, turkey, and veggies for 1 hour before cooking.
2. Pour 1/2 cup warm water over the chutney leather and raisins. Set aside while making the curry.
3. Boil 3 cups water and add the presoaked rice, turkey, and veggies. Reduce the heat and simmer for 15 minutes.
4. Taste and add the extra curry or chile to refresh flavors as needed.
5. If the ingredients need extra time to soften, cover the pot and set aside for 10 minutes. Reheat briefly before serving.
6. Top your bowl of curry and rice with a dollop of chutney.

SOUTHERN HOPPIN' JOHN

Hoppin' John is a rice dish normally made with sausage. This version uses lean buffalo. You can substitute buffalo jerky in all recipes that call for beef jerky.

1/4 cup dehydrated rice blend
1/4 cup dehydrated black-eyed peas
1/4 cup red wine buffalo jerky
1 package Basic Veggie Blend
2 to 4 cups water
Red chile flakes to taste
1 teaspoon extra-virgin olive oil
Salt and pepper to taste
1 tablespoon dehydrated onion

In Camp

1. Presoak the rice blend, black-eyed peas, buffalo jerky, and veggies for 1 hour before cooking.

2. Boil the 2 to 4 cups water and add the presoaked rice blend, peas, buffalo, and veggie blend. Cook for 10 to 15 minutes covered.

3. Add extra chile flakes to taste.

4. Drizzle with the olive oil, sprinkle with the salt and pepper and top with the dehydrated onion.

LEMON PEPPER BEEF AND BARLEY STEW

The combination of tart lemon and spicy pepper livens up this warming and filling meal. Add some dehydrated onion or Cheese Crisps on top for a little extra flavor and crunch.

1/8 cup lemon pepper beef jerky
1/4 cup dehydrated barley
1/4 cup Basic Veggie Blend
1/4 cup dehydrated potatoes
3 cups water
1 cube vegetable bouillon
1 teaspoon dried lemon zest
Extra ground black pepper to taste

1. Presoak the beef, barley, veggies, and potatoes together for 1 hour before cooking.

2. Boil the 3 cups water and dissolve the bouillon cube.

3. Add the presoaked beef, barley, veggies, potatoes, and zest. Reduce the heat and simmer for 10 to 15 minutes.

4. If the ingredients need more time to soften, set the pan aside for 10 minutes and then reheat briefly.

5. Serve the stew in two bowls with an extra sprinkle of ground pepper on top.

LAMB COUSCOUS WITH CRAN-RASP-BLACKBERRY MINT SAUCE

There is no tastier combo than lamb and mint. This trail version adds quick-cooking couscous as a base and vitamin C-rich Cran-

Rasp-Blackberry Mint Sauce to top it off. Hiking on Thanksgiving? Use turkey jerky and plain cranberry sauce.

1/8 cup red wine lamb jerky
1/4 cup Basic Veggie Blend
3 1/2 cups water
1 or 2 rolls Cran-Rasp-Blackberry Mint Leather
1 package (10 ounces) couscous
1 teaspoon dried mint
1 cube vegetable bouillon

In Camp

1. Presoak the lamb and veggies for 1 hour before cooking.

2. Add 1/2 cup hot water to the Cran-Rasp-Blackberry Mint Leather. Let sit until it forms a sauce-like consistency.

3. Cook couscous according to package instructions, set aside.

4. Boil 3 cups of water. Add the presoaked lamb and veggies and the mint and bouillon. Simmer for 10 minutes.

5. Turn off the heat. Add the couscous, mix briefly, cover, and let sit for 10 minutes.

6. Serve in two bowls with a dollop of the sauce from the rehydrated Cran-Rasp-Blackberry Mint Leather.

Soups

Cheese biscuits are delicious with these soups.

CHEESE BISCUITS

Makes 4 biscuits.

At Home

1 cup flour of choice
1/4 to 1/3 cup powdered whole milk
2 teaspoons baking powder
1/4 teaspoon salt

Combine all the ingredients and store in a labeled zip baggie.

In Camp

1/4 cup Cheese Crisps
1/2 cup water
2 tablespoons ghee

1. Add the Cheese Crisps and the water to the dry biscuit mix. Combine until you have a thick, sticky dough, then roll it into two balls.
2. Melt the ghee in a pan and press the balls into it until they are about 1/2 inch thick.
3. Cover the pan and cook on medium heat for 4 minutes on each side.

To vary the flavor, add sun-dried tomatoes, crushed nuts, garlic, and/or onion flakes to the dough before cooking the biscuits.

SPICY TOASTED PECAN SOUP WITH CHEESE CRISPS

Make this soup for a dinner at home, and then dry two or three servings as Soup Bark. In camp add extra dried onion, garlic, and red chile flakes to refresh the flavor. Just before serving, sprinkle the Cheese Crisps on top.

2 1/2 cups pecan halves
2 tablespoons extra-virgin olive oil
1 large onion, chopped
2 cloves garlic, minced
1/4 cup agave nectar
1 tablespoon chili powder
3 cups low-sodium chicken broth
4 sprigs fresh thyme
Salt and pepper to taste
4 cups water
1 cup organic low-fat milk or soymilk
1/4 cup Cheese Crisps
2 tablespoons dehydrated onion (optional)

1 teaspoon dehydrated garlic
1 teaspoon red chile flakes or to taste
Cheese Biscuits, for accompaniment

At Home

1. Preheat the oven to 350°F. Spread the pecans on a baking sheet and toast for 7 to 10 minutes, or until browned and aromatic. Let cool and then chop coarsely.

2. Warm the oil is a saucepan over medium heat. Add the onion and garlic; sauté until they are until soft. Add the chopped pecans, agave, and chili powder, and cook for 2 to 3 minutes. Add the broth, thyme, salt and pepper to taste, and the 4 cups water. Bring to a boil, then reduce the heat and simmer for 2 hours.

3. Remove the thyme sprigs, and puree the soup in a blender with the milk or soymilk.

4. Reheat the soup and serve half for dinner and dehydrate the other half as pecan soup bark for backpacking.

5. Package the pecan soup bark in two zip baggies.

In Camp

1. Over low heat, rehydrate 1 baggie of the pecan soup bark in 2 cups warm water, stirring slowly and adding water as needed until the bark is fully reconstituted.

2. Sprinkle with the Cheese Crisps and/or extra dehydrated onion, the dehydrated garlic, and red chile flakes to taste. If you prefer melted cheese, cover the pot and wait until the cheese is melted on top. Serve with the Cheese Biscuits.

CHUNKY TUNA CHOWDER

Chowder is especially warming and filling on a cool or rainy day.

1/2 cup Basic Veggie Blend
2 tablespoons ghee
2 cups water
1 teaspoon Italian seasoning blend

1/2 to 3/4 cup powdered whole milk
1/4 cup flour
Salt and ground black pepper to taste
1 foil pack (5 ounces) tuna

In Camp

1. Soak the Basic Veggie Blend in water for 1 hour before cooking.
2. Melt the ghee in a pan. Add the soaked veggies with 1 1/4 cups water. Bring to a boil, then reduce the heat and simmer, covered, for about 10 minutes.
3. In a small bowl combine the Italian seasoning blend, milk powder, flour, salt, and pepper. Gradually add 3/4 cup water and stir until smooth and thick. Add this mixture to the basic veggie mixture; blend well.
4. Fold in the tuna and heat through.

MULLIGATAWNY CURRY SOUP WITH RICE

British colonialists brought this soup back from India in the late 1700s. Mulligatawny literally means "pepper water." For this recipe, dehydrate extra root veggies: 1/2 turnip, 1 potato, and 2 carrots. Mix and package together in one baggie.

1/2 cup dehydrated rice blend
1/2 cup Indian chicken jerky
1/4 cup Indian Veggie Blend
1/2 cup dehydrated root veggies
4 whole cloves
6 peppercorns
3 to 4 cups water
1 cube vegetable bouillon
1 tablespoon curry powder
10 to 12 raisins

1. Presoak the rice blend, chicken, veggie blend, root veggies, cloves, and peppercorns for 1 hour before cooking.

2. Bring the 3 to 4 cups water to a boil and add the bouillon cube and the presoaked rice, chicken, veggie blend, and root veggies.
3. Add the curry and raisins and cook for 15 minutes.
4. If the rice, veggies, and chicken are not soft enough, cover the pan and let sit for 10 minutes. Then reheat briefly before serving.

SPLIT PEA SOUP WITH MUSHROOM BARLEY

Split pea soup is full of protein and fiber to fill up a hungry hiker. Some extra red chile flakes help keep the feet warm on a cool night in the mountains. This soup is especially good with Sunflower Flax Chips.

1/2 cup barley
1/2 cup Basic Veggie Blend
1/2 cup dried mushrooms
3 to 4 cups water
Baggie of split pea bark (equal to 1 bowl of soup)
1 tablespoon red chile flakes
Salt and pepper to taste

1. Presoak the barley, veggies, and mushrooms for 1 hour before cooking.
2. Bring the 3 to 4 cups water to a boil, and add the split pea bark. Stir until the bark is softened and blended.
3. Add the red chile flakes, salt and pepper, and the presoaked barley, veggies, and mushrooms. Cook for 15 minutes. If the barley, veggies, and mushrooms are not soft enough, cover the pan and let it sit for 10 minutes. Then reheat briefly before serving.

ITALIAN SALMON SOUP

1/2 cup dehydrated white beans
1 package Italian Veggie Blend
1/2 cup small pasta shells
2 to 4 cups water
2 rolls Tomato Sauce Leather
1 teaspoon Italian seasoning blend
1 foil pack (6 ounces) pink salmon

2 tablespoons olive oil
Shredded Parmesan cheese to taste

In Camp

1. Soak the beans and veggies for 1 hour before cooking.
2. Soak the pasta for 15 to 30 minutes or until soft before cooking.
3. Bring the water to a boil and add the beans, veggies, Tomato Sauce Leather, and Italian seasoning. Cook until the beans and veggies reach the desired consistency and the leather is a rich sauce.
4. Add the salmon and olive oil and cook until the salmon is hot.
5. Serve and sprinkle with the Parmesan cheese.

ASIAN-STYLE NOODLE SOUP

1 package Asian Veggie Blend
1/4 cup Asian chicken jerky
4 ounces dry flat rice noodles
2 to 4 cups water
1 teaspoon crushed dried mint
2 teaspoons olive oil

In Camp

1. Soak the Asian Veggie Blend and Asian chicken jerky for 30 minutes to 1 hour before cooking.

2. In a large bowl, pour enough hot water over the rice noodles to cover; let soak about 10 minutes to soften (or follow package instructions).

3. Bring the 2 to 4 cups water to a boil and add the Asian Veggie Blend, Asian chicken jerky, and the mint. Cook until the veggies and jerky are soft.

4. Drain the noodles. Add the veggies, jerky, and mint mixture. Toss with the olive oil and serve.

Pasta dishes

Although many cooks normally discard the pasta water to get rid of the starch, Italian chefs often use it to enrich and thicken their sauce. Because water and fuel conservation are a big part of backcountry food prep, unless I have a big campfire and lots of water, I soak the dehydrated pasta and then add it and its remaining liquid to all the other ingredients to warm them, thicken the sauce, and complete the dish. The sauce thus becomes extra rich and tasty.

SALMON AND UDON NOODLES IN MISO BROTH

This is my favorite dish on the trail. I like a miso soup brand that has some seaweed and tofu bits. Extra broken pieces of nori could be added to this meal for taste and minerals. Because the foil-packed salmon is a little heavy, I often include it in a resupply box halfway through a long trip as a special treat.

2 servings udon noodles
1/4 cup Asian Veggie Blend
3 to 4 cups water
2 single-serving packets of powdered miso soup
1 foil pack (8 ounces) wild salmon
1 sheet nori, cut into 1/2-inch strips

In Camp

1. Soak the udon noodles and veggies separately 30 minutes to 1 hour before cooking.

2. Bring the 3 to 4 cups water to a boil and add the miso powder, salmon, nori strips, and veggies. Simmer for 10 minutes, or until the miso is dissolved and the veggies are soft.

3. Add the soaked noodles and salmon and continue cooking for about 2 minutes or until they are hot.

4. Serve in two deep bowls and slurp.

LINGUINI AND TUNA WITH CHEDDAR CHEESE SAUCE

This is a hunger-busting one-pot tuna casserole.

2 servings dry linguini
1 1/2 cups Basic Veggie Blend
3 to 4 cups water
1 foil pack (6 ounces) tuna

CHEDDAR CHEESE SAUCE

1/4 cup powdered milk
1 cup warm water
1/2 cup Cheddar Cheese Crisps
Salt and pepper to taste

In Camp

1. Presoak the pasta and veggies separately 30 minutes to 1 hour before cooking.

2. Bring the 3 to 4 cups water to a boil and add the veggies. Reduce the heat and cook for 10 minutes.

3. To make the sauce, place the powdered milk in a mug or a small bowl. Add the warm water and stir until the milk has no lumps and is creamy. Slowly stir this mixture into the veggie mixture.

4. When the powdered milk is thoroughly dissolved, add the Cheese Crisps, salt, and pepper, and stir until the cheese is melted.

5. Add the presoaked pasta and tuna. Stir until it is coated with the creamy cheese sauce and the pasta is hot. Serve with a sprinkle of salt and ground pepper on top.

FUSILLI WITH SPINACH AND ASIAGO CHEESE

Asiago is a dry, hard cheese similar to Parmesan. It is excellent with crackers for lunch or pasta for dinner. Fusilli (corkscrew) is a meatier pasta than spaghetti and fills you up.

1 pound fresh organic spinach

4 cloves garlic, finely chopped
1/2 red onion, finely chopped
2 servings fusilli pasta
1 package Italian Veggie Blend
2 rolls Tomato Sauce Leather
1 teaspoon Italian seasoning blend
1/4 cup grated Asiago cheese
1/4 cup grated Parmesan cheese
1/8 cup olive oil
Salt and ground black pepper to taste

At Home

1. Dehydrate 1 pound fresh spinach.

2. Dehydrate 4 finely chopped garlic cloves and 1/2 red onion and package together in a zip baggie.

In Camp

1. Soak the fusilli for 30 minutes to 1 hour before cooking. Reserve the liquid.

2. Boil 2 to 3 cups water. Add the Italian veggies, dehydrated garlic and onion, and Tomato Sauce Leather and simmer for 10 minutes.

3. Add the dehydrated spinach and the Italian seasoning blend. Simmer for 5 more minutes.

4. Add the soaked fusilli pasta, Asiago, Parmesan, olive oil, salt, and pepper. Stir and warm about 2 more minutes until the pasta is hot. Serve.

THIN SPAGHETTI WITH CHICKEN, CHICKPEAS, SPINACH, AND MUSHROOMS

1/4 cup cooked and dehydrated chickpeas
1/2 cup dehydrated mushrooms
4 cloves garlic, dehydrated
1/2 red onion, dehydrated
6 pieces Italian chicken jerky

2 servings thin spaghetti (vermicelli)
3 to 4 cups water
1 cube chicken or vegetable bouillon (optional)
1 roll Tomato Sauce Leather
1 pound spinach, dehydrated
2 tablespoons Parmesan cheese

In Camp

1. Presoak the dehydrated chickpeas, mushrooms, garlic, onion, and chicken jerky for 1 hour before cooking.

2. Presoak the spaghetti for 15 to 30 minutes before preparing the meal.

3. Bring the 3 to 4 cups water to a boil. Add the presoaked chickpeas, mushrooms, garlic, onion, and chicken jerky. Add the bouillon (if used) and Tomato Sauce Leather and gently boil for 10 to 15 minutes or until the chickpeas are soft.

4. Add the presoaked spaghetti and dehydrated spinach. Simmer for 2 more minutes. Serve with Parmesan sprinkled on top.

Delectable Desserts

Desserts pump up the needed caloric intake after an arduous day on the trail. More than that, they offer a sweet reward for hard work. Some of these desserts[44] also can serve as breakfasts for a rest day in camp.

MANGO APPLE BREAD PUDDING

This recipe serves two.

1/2 cup seeded bread crumbs (dried from 2 slices seeded bread, each 1/2 inch thick)
2 tablespoons brown sugar
2 tablespoons ground cinnamon
1/8 cup chopped dried apple
1/8 cup chopped dried mango
10 Flame raisins
1/2 to 3/4 cup water
Sprinkle of crushed nuts or granola
Brown sugar (optional)

At Home

1. To make the bread crumbs, place the bread slices on a dehydrator tray, sprinkle with the brown sugar and cinnamon, and

dehydrate at 125°F for about 4 hours. Crumble the dried bread and pack in a zip baggie.

2. Pack the dried apples, mangos, and raisins together in a zip baggie.

In Camp

1. Bring the 1/2 to 3/4 cup water to a boil. Reduce the heat and add the dried fruit. Maintain a low flame until the fruit is soft and warm, about 5 to 10 minutes.

2. Stir in the prepared bread crumbs. Turn off the heat and let sit until the bread crumbs absorb the juices from the fruit.

3. Place the mixture in two bowls and sprinkle with the nuts, granola, or brown sugar as desired.

BLACK FOREST BROWNIE

This recipe serves one person although the package makes plenty of brownies for extra servings as well as a snack with tea in the afternoon.

1/8 cup water
1/8 cup chopped dried cherries
1 tablespoon dried orange zest
1 brownie (2 inches square)

At Home

Make your favorite dark chocolate brownies at home per your recipe or package instructions. (I like Ghirardelli dark chocolate brownie mix.) Add chopped hazelnuts and dark chocolate chips for an extra-decadent flavor. Cut the brownies into 2-inch-square pieces. Take a few on the trail for snacks and one per person for dessert in camp.

In Camp

1. Bring the 1/8 cup water to a boil. Add the cherries and orange zest and let sit until the cherries are soft and orange-scented.

2. Place the brownie on a plate and pour the warm cherries over the top. Let the fruit sauce soak in for a minute and then dig in.

CHOCOLATE-DIPPED CRYSTALLIZED GINGER

This serves two people. To serve more people, add an extra 2 ounces of chocolate, 1/2 teaspoon oil, and 2 pieces of ginger per person.

1 cup water
4 ounces semisweet baking chocolate
1 teaspoon coconut oil
4 pieces (3 to 4 inches long) crystallized ginger

1. Add the 1 cup water to a 1- or 2-liter pot. Place over medium heat until the water boils.

2. Make a double boiler by placing a metal cup in the water and adding the chocolate to the cup. As the chocolate starts to melt, pour in the oil. Stir until thoroughly mixed and melted.

3. Dip the ginger slices into the chocolate. Bite, dip, bite, dip, bite.

PUMPKIN APPLESAUCE

This recipe serves two people and can be a warm, tasty breakfast, too.

2 rolls pumpkin leather
1/4 cup chopped dried apples
3/4 to 1 cup warm water or as needed
1/4 cup powdered milk
1 cup granola
Brown sugar to taste
Chopped nuts (optional)

In Camp

1. Soak the pumpkin leather and dried apples in 1/2 cup warm water until they're soft.

2. Mix the powdered milk with 1/4 cup water or as needed to make it creamy.

3. Put two equal portions of granola in two bowls. Cover each with the warm pumpkin and apples and top with the milk, the brown sugar, and/or nuts.

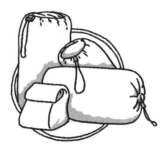

Packaging Food for a Hike

You will need:

~ Food scale
~ Resealable zip baggies – snack, sandwich, quart, and gallon sizes
~ Fine-tipped permanent marker for labeling

You will be measuring meal-size quantities into an assortment of baggies, and then using an indelible marker to label the meal with breakfast, lunch, or dinner; the name of the dish (chili); the day (#2); and the preparation instructions.

Weigh each prepared baggie as you go along. It helps to manage your overall pack weight, especially if you know you've included some expendable items such as an extra three chocolate bars or a pound of cashews. Remember: two pounds of food per person per day is the foundation. If you are out for five days, that will be ten pounds of food per person.

Here are a few strategies that help me keep things organized.

Packaging

It is best to use high-quality freezer baggies that will zip tightly and not pierce easily. These hold the presoaking water best. If they survive the journey, they can be reused after a wash at home. Do not leave them in the wild! Leave no trace!

For each meal, pack the ingredients you'll want to presoak (such as jerky, veggies, and grains) in separate baggies from ingredients that will cook quickly.

If you want to bring extra seasonings, put them in a little plastic spice bag and add them while the food is cooking. Sometimes I take a designated spice bag with an assortment of blends in their own little bags.

Keep perishables, Cheese Crisps, and powdered milk in separate baggies from other meal components.

Make sure that liquid oils are in tightly sealed plastic bottles and inserted into their own baggie. It is a huge mess if they leak all over everything else!

I also make a designated gallon-size snack food baggie.

Assembling

Assemble the components for each meal. Put the separate baggies for each component of a meal into a gallon baggie and label it. I make of note of instructions and presoaking needs on the outside of the big bag, too.

There are as many ways to pack your meals as there are human personality types. Some folks like to have all the components separate so they can mix and match meals as they feel inspired in camp. But because of presoaking, I like to have the ingredients preplanned and accessible.

I don't like to scramble through every pocket of my pack to find the meals, so I have a designated stuff sack that holds all labeled baggies. The food stuff sack is the last thing I put inside my pack, so it sits snugly—but not squished—on top of my other gear.

Labeling

There is room for great personal preference in how to package and label the meals. Forethought in when and how you want to access them for consumption is the key. My preferred style of organizing meals is labeling baggies for each meal according to the daily method. Others like the meal method or the grab bag method.

Daily method

Day 1 lunch, Day 1 dinner. All Day 1 meals fit into a one-gallon bag labeled Day 1 meals.

Day 2 breakfast, Day 2 lunch, Day 2 dinner. All Day 2 meals fit into a one-gallon bag labeled Day 2 meals.

And so on.

Meal method

Three one-gallon bags: one for dinners, one for lunches, and one for breakfasts, with each meal packed in a smaller bag inside the bigger bags. Then you can choose which meal you want for each day as you go along.

Grab bag method

The food is sorted into gallon bags that are labeled according to the category, such as veggies, jerky, grains, pantry, et cetera. Ingredients that are needed to assemble each meal can be grabbed as desired.

I put assorted snacks into a one-gallon baggie except for a small quantity that goes into the pocket on my waist belt for quick access every time a steep ascent looms or is behind me.

Tip: Remember to take these snacks out of your waist belt or fanny pack and hang them in the bear bag at night along with the rest of the food.

Lunch packaging can sometimes be more varied because I might have one box of crackers that I place somewhere they won't get crushed; some fresh radishes, cheese, or sprouts that I tuck next to the water bladder in my pack to keep them cool; and some hummus or tabouli that need hydrating before lunch.

Tip: For those spur-of-the-moment hikes, prepare an extra meal every time you make planned meals for planned hikes. Dehydrated food stores for several months in the cupboard and a year in the fridge or freezer.

Trail's End

When I tell people that I didn't begin backpacking until I was fifty-eight years old and that I have since hiked for as many as a hundred consecutive miles through the mountains, they look at me with disbelief. Some people give up on their bodies at a much younger age. Here are two reasons why I can accomplish these treks.

First, I am not competitive, rushed, or anxious. I take hiking as an opportunity to contemplate the wonders of our stunning planet away from the frenetic pace of modern life. In that frame of mind, the miles fall behind me like the wake of a boat on a quiet lake. It is not the distances that matter; it is the calm. So I suggest that you plan a backpacking adventure that is right for you. It may be simply a mile to a waterfall or many days in the wild. The important thing is to share in this relationship with the natural world.

Second, I take care of my nutritional needs with gentle but persistent attention. I love to eat. Planning for the meals I'll savor in the backcountry is my idea of fun! If I consume junk food, my body rebels; if I eat right, rest when I'm tired, and plan with forethought, I am rewarded with good health, energy, and a sense of well-being. I can literally walk miles and miles.

That is why I have offered you this blueprint for creating ultra food for the trail. You should now be able to adapt any of your favorite recipes for ultra fun and ultra energy on ultra hikes! At the trail's end, you'll be ready to turn around and begin again.

Notes

1. Check wildland fire restrictions in your area at http://199.134.225.62/FireRestrictions/index.htm.
2. You can calculate your backpacking calories burned at http://www.sparkpeople.com/resource/calories_burned.asp.
3. There are several informative web sites about lightweight backpacking, including http://www.hikelight.com, http://www.gofastandlight.com, and http://www.backpackinglight.com/.
4. For thorough information on nutritional data with multiple reliable references, I go to http://www.whfoods.com. This site is sponsored by the George Mateljan Foundation, a not-for-profit foundation with no commercial interests or advertising.
5. www.springerlink.com/index/M4070343V7465672.pdf; www.ncbi.nlm.nih.gov/pmc/articles/.../pdf/brjsmed00034-0032.pdf; and www.fao.org/docrep/w8079e/w8079e0n.htm.
6. http://michaelpollan.com/articles-archive/you-are-what-you-grow/.
7. R. Knopp and B. Retzlaff. Saturated fat prevents coronary artery disease? An American paradox. *American Journal of Clinical Nutrition*, Vol. 80, No. 5, 1102–3, November 2004.
8. www.framinghamheartstudy.org.
9. http://www.ajcn.org/cgi/content/abstract/86/2/353.

10. http://www.reuters.com/article/idUSN2013098020100420.

11. http://www.livestrong.com/article/250346-parmesan-cheese-nutrition/#ixzz1RXloTiJ6.

12. For an excellent and detailed description of purification options, go to http://zenbackpacking.net/WaterFilterPurifierTreatment.htm.

13. http://www.bt.cdc.gov/radiation/ki.asp.

14. "Take the leisurely pace of most hikes and multiply it by 10. Now take the pack you typically carry, and lighten it to about 10-15 lbs. That's fastpacking!" http://usparks.about.com/od/backcountry/a/Fastpacking.htm.

15. If your hike will last longer than five to ten days, you will have to resupply along the trail, partly so you do not carry too much weight and partly to replenish fuel and repair gear. There are four popular methods of resupply: (1) to buy the things you need in towns near the trail you are hiking; (2) to send yourself a box at a post office near the trail; (3) to hike in to various drop spots or trailheads along the way ahead of the hike dates and hide a box (or ask a ranger station attendant to keep it); or (4) to have a support person or team to bring you supplies. Most hikers opt for a combination of these methods. Your box will include food, cooking fuel, fresh clothes as needed, and personal treats and needs. For more details, go to http://planetanimals.com/logue/resupply.html.

16. http://journeytoforever.org/edu_bkpkstove.html.

17. http://www.banthebottle.net/articles/battle-of-the-reusable-bottles-plastic-vs-aluminum-vs-stainless-steel/.

18. For a free complete nutritional analysis of any recipe in this book, copy the ingredients into http://caloriecount.about.com/cc/recipe_analysis.php.

19. http://www.mayoclinicproceedings.org/article/S0025-6196%2812%2900473-9/abstract.

20. http://www.usatoday.com/news/health/2009-02-11-protein-recovery_N.htm.

21. http://www.eatwild.com/healthbenefits.htm.

22. http://www.care2.com/greenliving/9-gluten-free-grains.html#ixzz20Q3AIoaG.

23. For a thorough study and review of various antioxidants and their influence on exercise recovery, go to http://www.exrx.net/Nutrition/Antioxidants/Antioxidants.html.

24. http://www.monasteryfruitcake.org/productsfraters.asp.

25. For an in-depth analysis of each of these foods, go to http://www.whfoods.com/.

26. G. Howatson, et al. Influence of tart cherry juice on indices of recovery following marathon running. *Scandanavian Journal of Medical Science*, 2009.

27. At any single meal, we rarely eat a great enough quantity of spice to equal laboratory-induced benefits, but taken as a regular part of our diet, the cumulative effect of herbs and spices, along with nutrient-rich foods, is beneficial.

28. K. C. Srivastava and T. Mustafa. Ginger (Zingiber officinale) in rheumatism and musculoskeletal disorders. *Medical Hypotheses*, 1992 Dec.; 39(4): 342–8.

29. P. Zoladz, B. Raudenbush, and S. Lilley. Cinnamon perks performance. Paper presented at the annual meeting of the Association for Chemoreception Sciences, held in Sarasota, FL, April 21–25, 2004.

30. B. Bryson, *A Walk in the Woods: Rediscovering America on the Appalachian Trail*. Broadway, 1999.

31. http://www.rei.com/search?query=backpacking+food.

32. http://nutritiondata.self.com/topics/processing.

33. http://preparedforthat.com/how-to-freeze-dry-food-at-home/.

34. http://www.webmd.com/food-recipes/news/20090323/7-rules-for-eating.

35. http://wholenewmom.com/whole-new-budget/which-costs-the-least-dehydrating-freezing-or-canning/.

36. http://www.dehydratorbook.com/homemade-dehydrator.html.

37. Calculate calories at http://www.ichange.com/nutrition/.

38. http://www.nrdc.org/health/effects/mercury/tuna.asp.

39. For a free complete nutritional analysis of any recipe in this book, copy the ingredients into http://caloriecount.about.com/cc/recipe_analysis.php.

40. http://books.google.com/books?id=Ea6goJ0LVIAC&pg=PA24&dq=cr
unchy+endorphins&hl=en&sa=X&ei=FRb7UMOfO8bqqQGYuo-
HIDg&ved=0CDYQ6AEwAQ#v=onepage&q=crunchy%20endor-
phins&f=false.

41. For a free complete nutritional analysis of any recipe in this book,
copy the ingredients into
http://caloriecount.about.com/cc/recipe_analysis.php.

42. For a free complete nutritional analysis of any recipe in this book,
copy the ingredients into
http://caloriecount.about.com/cc/recipe_analysis.php.

43. For a free complete nutritional analysis of any recipe in this book,
copy the ingredients into
http://caloriecount.about.com/cc/recipe_analysis.php.

44. For a free complete nutritional analysis of any recipe in this book,
copy the ingredients into
http://caloriecount.about.com/cc/recipe_analysis.php.

References

Bell, Mary T. *Food Drying with an Attitude: A Fun and Fabulous Guide to Creating Snacks, Meals, and Crafts*. New York: Skyhorse Publishing, 2008.

————. *Mary Bell's Complete Dehydrator Cookbook*. New York: William Morrow, 1994.

DeLong, Deanna. *How to Dry Foods*. Tucson, AZ: H.P. Books, 1979.

Densley, Barbara. *The ABC's of Home Food Dehydration*. Bountiful, Utah: Horizon Publishers, 1975.

Hobson, Phyllis. *Making & Using Dried Foods*. Vermont: Storey Books, 1994.

Kesselheim, Alan S. *Trail Food: Drying and Cooking Food for Backpacking and Paddling*. New York: McGraw Hill/Ragged Mountain Press, 1998.

MacKenzie, Jennifer, Jay Nutt, and Don Mercer. *The Dehydrator Bible: Includes over 400 Recipes*. Toronto, Canada: Robert Rose, 2009.

Popeil, Ron. *Dehydrated & Delicious: The Complete Book on Dehy-*

drating Meats, Fruits, Vegetables, Herbs, Flowers, Yogurt, and More. Carlsbad, CA: Dehydrator Products, 1993.

Suzanne, Kristen. *Kristen Suzanne's EASY Raw Vegan Dehydrating: Delicious & Easy Raw Food Recipes for Dehydrating Fruits, Vegetables, Nuts, Seeds, Pancakes, Crackers, Breads, Granola, Bars & Wraps.* Scottsdale, AZ: Green Butterfly Press, 2009.

Yaffe, Linda Frederick. *Backpack Gourmet: Good Hot Grub You Can Make at Home, Dehydrate, and Pack for Quick, Easy, and Healthy Eating on the Trail.* Mechanicsburg, PA: Stackpole Books, 2002.

Index

A

aerobic exercise, 8–9
aerobic metabolism, 8, 40
anti-inflammatories. see inflammation
antioxidants, 33, 35, 36, 38
    health benefits of, 33, 38, 40, 69

B

bark, soup, 54. *see also* soup bark
blood sugar, 8, 31–32, 36, 40
    high, 32
    low, 8, 43
bowls, camping, 27–28
breakfasts, 71–76
    Breakfast Oat-Nut Cookie, 73
    Hot Apple Almond Quinoa Cereal,
        76
    Hot Rice Pudding, 72–73
    Hot Sprouted Buckwheat Muesli, 71
    Instant Grits with Nuts, Dried Fruit,
        and Ghee, 72
    Sunflower Seed Pancake Fruit Jam
        Wrap, 74
    Warm Pumpkin Granola Crisp, 75–
        76
butter, 12, 13. *see also* ghee

C

calories, 11
    adding extra to meals, 45
    amount burned hiking, 4, 43

and disease, 12–13
    in fats, 11
    in grains, 32
carbohydrates. see CHOs
cheeses, 16, 59
    Cheddar Cheese Sauce, 94
    Cheese Biscuits, 87–88
    Cheese Crisps, 59–60
    Parmesan as good choice of, 13–14
chocolate:
    best types to choose or avoid, 40
    health benefits of, 40
    Mocha Mix, 68
CHOs, 7
    effects of depletion of, 8
    and endurance, 10
    refined, effects of, 31–32
    stored as glycogen, 8
coffee, 67–68
    Mocha Mix, 68
crackers:
    Cajun Flax Almond, 57
    Cheese Crisps, 58
    Southwest Flax, 58
    Sunflower Flax, 58

D

dehydrated foods, 41–47
    advantages of, 41–42
    compared to other preservation
        methods, 41–43

packaged vs. homemade, 41, 43
portion sizes of, 44, 45
rehydrating. see rehydrating foods
storing. see storing dehydrated foods
techniques for making, 44–47. *see also* specific food types
dehydration (in humans), 16–17
desserts, 97–100
  Black Forest Brownie, 98–99
  Chocolate-Dipped Crystallized Ginger, 99
  Mango Apple Bread Pudding, 97–98
  Pumpkin Applesauce, 99–100
diet:
  and endurance. see endurance
  and energy. see energy (human)
  and exercise. see exercise
dinners, 81–96. *see also* soups
  Black Rice Curry with Turkey and Chutney, 84–85
  Black-Eyed Buffalo Chili, 83
  Cuban Black Beans with Rice, 84
  Lamb Couscous with Cran-Rasp-Blackberry Mint Sauce, 86–87
  Lemon Pepper Beef and Barley Stew, 86
  Mexican Bean Soup with Rice and Spicy Beef, 81–82
  Middle Eastern Red Lentils with Turkey, 82–83
  Southern Hoppin' John, 85–86
diseases:
  and fats, 11, 12, 13, 15
  and processed foods, 29
  and sugar, 11
dishes, camping, 27–28
dried foods. see dehydrated foods
drinks, 67–69. *see also* fluids; water
  coffee, 67–68
    Mocha Mix, 68
  instant, 69
  teas, 68–69
drying foods. see dehydrated foods

E
eggs, benefits of, 16
electrolytes, 63, 69
  described, 17–18
  in Emergen-C, 67, 69
  in free-range meats, 31
  function of, 17, 35
  good food choices for, 18, 61, 65–66, 67, 69
endurance:
  good food choices for, 10–11
    eggs, 16
  and high CHO diet, 9
  water and, 16
energy (human), 3, 5, 7–18
  effects of aerobic exercise on, 8–9
  effects of diet on, 9, 30, 34
exercise. *see also* recovery after exercise
  beneficial forms of, 8
  and diet, 7, 9
  and effects on the body, 7–18

F
fatigue, 8, 10, 11, 30, 35
fats:
  function of, 12
  good choices of, 13, 14, 15
  good vs. bad, 11
  monounsaturated, described, 14
  polyunsaturated, described, 14
  saturated,
    described, 13
    good choices of, 15
  trans, described, 13, 14–15
fiber, 34, 35, 36, 37
  health benefits of, 32, 36
fish, 15, 48. *see also* seafood

dehydrating, 47, 48
healthy choices of, 31
fluids, 16–17. *see also* drinks; water
foods. *see also* specific food types
    best types to eat for hiking, 9
    daily amount hikers should take, 4
    dehydrated. see dehydrated foods
    packaged. see packaged foods
    processed. see processed foods
    to avoid, 35, 36, 37, 38, 40
fruit leathers, 51–52
    Cran-Rasp-Blackberry Mint Sauce, 52
    Indian Chutney, 52
fruits, 46, 50–51. *see also* fruit leathers
    best to choose or avoid, 33, 36–37
    dehydrating, 51
    drying temperature, 47
    Fruit Jam, 74
    health benefits of, 34, 36–37
    prep for drying, 46

G
ghee, 13, 15, 62–63
glucose, 8. *see also* blood sugar; glycogen
glycogen, 8
    and CHOs, 8
    effects of depletion during exercise, 8
    and glucose, 8
    replacing after exercise, 9
GMOs, 33
grains. *see also* whole grains
    dehydrating, 55
    rehydrating, 24

H
herbs and spices, 61–62. *see also* spices
hydration. *see also* dehydration (in humans)
    amount to drink when hiking, 23, 67
    importance of, 17
    systems of, 22–23
hypoglycemia. see glycogen

I
immune system, 10, 36, 37
inflammation, 13, 31, 33, 35
    anti-inflammatories for, 15, 32, 36, 38, 39
injuries, caused by improper food or hydration, 8, 16–17

J
jerky, 47–48, 50
    best protein to use for, 47–48
    drying, 50
    marinating. see marinades
    prep for making, 48
    rehydrating, 24
    storing, 50–51
joints, 16, 31, 32, 36, 37, 57

L
leathers, 51–54
    Cran-Rasp-Blackberry Mint Sauce, 52
    How to make, 51
    Indian chutney, 52
    Salsa, 53
    Tomato sauce, 53
liver (human organ), 8
    and glucose, 8
lunches, 77–80
    7 day menu, 79–80
    Basic Homemade Dehydrated Hummus, 78–79

M
macronutrients, described, 7
marinades, 46, 48–50
    basic, 49
    homemade Worcestershire sauce, 48
    Indian, 49
    Lemon Pepper, 49
    Mexican Spicy, 50

Red Wine, 50
meats:
    dehydrating, 46, 47, 48
    health benefits of free-range, 31
micronutrients, 7, 10, 17, 18, 29, 32,
        33, 44
minerals, 17
    in dark, leafy greens, 36
    in Emergen-C, 69
    in fruits, 34, 37
    in grains, 35
    in nori, 93
    in nuts, 15, 38
muscles, 35. *see also* recovery after
        exercise
    aches and pains, 8, 10, 16–17, 35,
        37, 69
    energy supply to, 7–8
    and importance of protein, 10

N
nutrition, basic concepts of, 7–18
nuts and nut butters, 14, 15
    best to choose or avoid, 38
    health benefits of, 38

O
oils, 14
    cooking, 62
    ghee, 62–63
    from nuts, 14
    olive, benefits of, 15
    omega-3 and omega-6, 14
    good choices of, 14, 31, 38, 57
oxygen, and exercise, 8

P
packaged foods, 62
packing meals, 101–103
pastas, 55, 93–96
    dehydrating, 55
    Fusilli with Spinach and Asiago

Cheese, 94–95
    Linguini and Tuna with Cheddar
        Cheese Sauce, 94
    Salmon and Udon Noodles in Miso
        Broth, 93
    Thin Spaghetti with Chicken,
        Chickpeas, Spinach, and Mush-
        rooms, 95–96
plates, camping, 27–28
poultry:
    dehydrating, 48
    health benefits of cage-free, 31
prep time for making ultra foods, 5
processed foods, 29, 36
    fats and disease and, 11, 12, 13, 42
protein, 10
    ailments caused by lack of, 10
    function of, 10, 30
    good choices of, 10–11

R
real food, 7, 43
    vs. supplements, 10, 30, 34
recovery after exercise, 9, 11, 30
    good food choices for, 15, 16, 35,
        37, 39–40, 69
refined foods. see CHOs; whole grains
rehydrating foods, 24, 47

S
seafood, 4. *see also* fish
    dehydrating, 48, 50
    healthy choices of, 31
    storing, 50
snacks, 65–67
    electrolyte rich, 65–66
    high energy, 34
    protein bars, 67
    Simple Crunchy Granola Bars, 66
    Ultra Trail Mix, 66
soup bark, 54
soups, 54, 87–92

Asian-Style Noodle, 92
Chunky Tuna Chowder, 89–90
Italian Salmon, 91–92
Mulligatawny Curry with Rice, 90–91
Spicy Toasted Pecan with Cheese Crisps, 88–89
Split Pea with Mushroom Barley, 91
spices, 61–62
    best to choose, 39–40
    healing, 39
    in marinades, 46
storing dehydrated foods, 47, 103
storing jerky, 50–51
stoves, camp, 25–27
    canisters, 25, 26
    denatured alcohol, 26–27
    Esbit pocket stoves, 25–26
    liquid-fuel, 25–26
    white-gas, 26
sugar, 32. see also blood sugar
    illnesses related to, 11, 13, 32
sweeteners, 62

T
teas, 68–69
    for aches and pains, 68, 69
    as antioxidants, 69
    for digestion, 68
thinking and judgement, 8, 17, 38, 40, 43
treats, 34. see also snacks
triglycerides, 13

U
ultra foods, 30
    best to choose, 34–40
    criteria for, 4
    described, 4, 30

utensils, camping, 4, 27

V
vegetables:
    best to choose or avoid, 33, 36, 77
    dehydrating, 47
    health benefits of, 36
vegetarian diet, 31
    vegan jerky, 47–48
Veggie Blends, 56
    Asian, 56
    Basic Stew, 56
    Indian (east), 56
    Italian, 56
    Mexican Spicy, 56
viruses, removing from water, 19, 20, 22, 24
vitamins, 9, 33, 42, 69
    in cheeses, 16
    in eggs, 16
    in Emergen-C, 69
    and fats, 12
    in fruits and vegetables, 34, 36, 37
    in nuts, 15, 38
    in spices, 39–40

W
water. see also fluids
    amount to drink when hiking, 23, 67
    physiological necessity for, 16–17
    purification methods of, 19–24
    removing viruses from. see viruses
weight gain, 8, 11, 32
weight loss, 7, 8
whole grains. see also grains
    best to choose or avoid, 35
    health benefits of, 32, 35
    vs. refined, 32

About the Author:

Cinny Green is a writer, editor, avid backpacker, and back country guide in Santa Fe, NM. She was editorial manager for a website on healing foods called myhealingkitchen.com. Cinny also received a Masters in Humanities with concentration on ecological writing from Prescott College. Her thesis was entitled *The Wild Writer*. She was 2d place winner of 2009 LAURA Award, *Woman Writing the West*. Her book TRAIL WRITER's GUIDE won the *Foreward Magazine* Book of the Year Bronze award, and was finalist in the New Mexico Book Association Southwest Book Design and Production Award.

Also by Cinny Green

TRAIL WRITER'S GUIDE
Cinny Green
Illustrated by Maureen Burdock
ISBN: 978-1-889921-50-1

$20.00 Includes postage and handling

Order from
Western Edge Press
126 Candelario St.
Santa Fe, NM 87501

Or online: www.westernedgepress.com

The beautifully illustrated *Trail Writer's Guide* offers more than fifty writing exercises to explore your moments of inspiration crossing forest paths, mountain creeks, or alpine tundra. Using actual trail stories, melded with her writing workshop experience, the fun writing lessons include themes of Dialogue, Conflict, Animal Imagery, Telling Details, Myth and Story, Character, and Resolution.

"I'm often asked how to write about walking in the wilderness. This unique book has the answers. Weaving ideas about writing with stories of walking, the author's words inspire and encourage. All who wish to express their love of wild places in words can learn from it."

—Chris Townsend, *The Backpacker's Handbook*